The Priest, The Woman

and

The Confessional

By CHINIQUY

_____

ISBN: 0-937958-03-4

CONTENTS

THROUGHOUT HISTORY, GOD HAS CALLED MEN AND WOMEN SUCH AS SAVONAROLA, JOHN HUSS, MARTIN LUTHER, KATHERINE VON BORA, CHINIQUY, SISTER CHARLOTTE AND MANY OTHERS, OUT OF THE ROMAN SYSTEM. EVEN TODAY ROMAN CATHOLICS ARE FINDING THE LIVING CHRIST.

THEY HAVE ONE THING IN COMMON: A HUNGER TO REALLY KNOW GOD AND THE TRUTH OF THE BIBLE. WHEN THE LIGHT OF GOD'S TRUTH HITS THEM, THEY KNOW THEY MUST DO WHAT THE BIBLE DEMANDS ... *"Come out of her, my people ... Revelation 18:4-5*

THE ROMAN CATHOLIC SYSTEM OR ITS POLICIES (DOGMAS) WILL **NEVER** CHANGE! THE ACTIVITIES CHINIQUY DESCRIBES IN THIS BOOK ARE STILL GOING ON. WITHOUT KNOWLEDGE THE PEOPLE PERISH.

MAY THIS BOOK OPEN YOUR MIND TO SEE THE DIFFERENCE BETWEEN RELIGION AND TRUE CHRISTIANITY.

YOURS FOR THE SALVATION OF THE
ROMAN CATHOLIC PEOPLE,

DR. ALBERTO RIVERA
(EX-JESUIT PRIEST)

WHO IS CHINIQUY?

IMPORTANT ORIGINAL DOCUMENTS

ESTABLISHING THE HIGH CHARACTER AND STANDING OF PASTOR CHINIQUY WHEN IN THE CHURCH OF ROME.

M R. CHINIQUY is one of the most conspicuous champions of Protestantism of the present day. He was invited to Scotland by her leading ecclesiastics to take part in the Tercentenary of the Reformation, and to England in later years, when all her leading Protestants stood forth to honor the Emperor William of Germany and Prince Bismarck for their noble resistance to Papal pretensions to authority in Germany. He then, in 1874, addressed the great gathering in Exeter Hall, over which Lord Russell presided; and afterwards, for six months, lectured throughout England on the invitation of Ministers of every Evangelical Denomination.

Of such a man with such a history of struggles, services and success, the Protestants all over the world need not be ashamed.

During the last two years he has lectured and preached to crowded houses in Australia, receiving from the clergy and people of that country many testimonials of their esteem and regard for his valuable services in the cause of Protestantism.

It is well known that Father Chiniquy rose into general notoriety in Canada as an Apostle of Temperance. But long before this—when a parish priest, and even when a student—he was held in high repute. The sketch of his early life is as follows: Born at Kamouraska, Canada, July 30, 1809. His father's name, Charles Chiniquy, his mother's, Reine Perrault, both natives of Quebec. His father died in 1821; his mother in 1830. After his father's death, a rich uncle, by name Amable Dionne, a member of the upper House of Parliament in Canada, who had married his mother's sister, took him in charge, and sent him to the College of St. Nicholet, with which he was connected from 1822 to 1833, attaining high honors as a linguist and mathematician. His moral conduct got him the name among his fellow-students of St. Louis Gonzaque de Nicholet. He was ordained a priest in 1833, in the Cathedral of Quebec, by Bishop Sinaie, and began his ministry at St. Charles, on the river Berger, Canada. After this he was Chaplain to the Marine Hospital, and there studied under Dr. Douglas the effects of alcohol on the human system. He became convinced that it was poisonous, and its general use criminal. He wrote to Father Matthew, of Ireland, and soon after started the Temperance Crusade among the Roman Catholics of Canada. He began at Beauport, where he was parish priest. There were then seven taverns or hotels, but no school. In two years he had seven schools, and not a single tavern in the parish. A Temperance Column was erected in that town to commemorate his achievements in this good work. He was soon transferred to the larger parish of Kamouraska; but he shortly gave up his parish duties and transferred his headquarters to Montreal, to devote his whole time to the cause of temperance,—from 1846 to 1851. As the result, all the distilleries were closed except two in the whole Province.

These noble efforts were publicly acknowledged. We refer to four distinct acts of recognition among many. The first is the Address of the Independent Order of Rechabites of Canada, and dated Montreal, 31st August, 1848, with Mr. Chiniquy's reply. It is creditable to the Protestants of Lower Canada that they so honored a priest of the Church of Rome when doing a noble work for the general good of the country. Both documents are worthy of the cause. Instead of taking glory to himself for this success, Mr. Chiniquy uses these words in the course of his reply: "Persuaded that this success is solely the work of God—to Him be all the glory!" The great city of Montreal was moved to gratitude, and a Gold Medal was presented to him in the name of the city, with these words on one side—

To FATHER CHINIQUY,
APOSTLE OF TEMPERANCE,
CANADA

And on the other—
HONOR TO HIS VIRTUES,
ZEAL AND PATRIOTISM.

The Canadian Parliament moved also in his honor, and voted to him an Address and Five Hundred Pounds as a public token of the gratitude of a whole people.

The fame of his labors in the cause of Temperance reached the Pope, and through an aspiring priest who visited Rome about that period, the Pope's Blessing was sent to Mr. Chiniquy, as testified by the following letter. The translations are verbatim, no freedom being taken to render them into more idiomatic English:—

[TRANSLATION]

"Rome, 10th August, 1850.

"Sir, and very Dear Friend:
"It is only Monday, the 12th, that it has been given me to have a private audience with the Sovereign Pontiff. I have taken the opportunity to present to him your book, with your letter, which he has received—

I do not say with that goodness which is so eminently characteristic—but with all special marks of satisfaction and of approbation, while charging me to state to you that HE ACCORDS HIS APOSTOLIC BENEDICTION TO YOU and to the holy work of Temperance which you preach.

"I esteem myself happy to have had to offer on your behalf to the Vicar of Jesus Christ, a book which, after it had done so much good to my countrymen, has been able to draw from his venerable mouth such solemn words of approbation of the Temperance Society, and of blessing on those who are its apostles; and it is also for my heart a very sweet pleasure to transmit them to you.

"Your friend,

"CHARLES T. BAILLARGEON,
"*Priest.*"

Following this we give the general circular furnished to him by the Bishop of Montreal, in which he is designated Apostle of Temperance.

[TRANSLATION]

IGNATIUS BOURGET.

"By the divine mercy and grace of the Holy Apostolic See, Bishop of Marianopolis (Montreal).

"To all who would inspect the present Letter we make known and testify:—That the venerable Charles Chiniquy, Apostle of Temperance, Priest of our Diocese, is very well known to us, and regard him as proved to lead a praiseworthy life and one agreeable to his ecclesiastical profession—through the tender mercies of our God under no ecclesiastical censures, at least which have come to our knowledge, by which he might be restricted. We entreat each and all Archbishops, Bishops and other dignitaries of the Church, to whom it may happen that he may go, that they for the love of Christ entertain him kindly and courteously, and as often as they may be asked by him, permit him to celebrate the Holy Sacrifice of the Mass, and exercise other ecclesiastical privileges and works of piety. We showing ourselves ready for similar and greater things. In confidence of which we have ordered the present general Letter to be prepared under our sign and seal, and with the subscription of the secretary of our Episcopate at Marianople, in our Palace of the Blessed James, in the year one thousand eight hundred and fifty, on the sixth day of the month of June.

"† IGNATIUS,
"*Bishop of Marianopolis.*

"By order of the most illustrious and most reverend Bishop of Marianopolis, D.D.

"J. O. PARE, Canon,
"*Secretary.*"

His high position was now universally acknowledged, and he was chosen by the dignitaries of the Church of Rome to lead a new and important movement. It was to take possession of the Valley of the Mississippi, and form a new Roman Catholic colony in the very centre of the United States. The Roman Catholic Bishop of Chicago, Bishop Vandevelt, came to Canada to confer with him on the subject. The proposal was to transfer thousands of French Canadians, zealous Roman Catholics, to this new territory, and Father Chiniquy was to conduct the enterprise and be the new champion of Rome. He accepted the offer. He went and surveyed the land, selected the territory, and returning to Canada took over to the new colony a first batch of five thousand emigrants, all zealous for the Church in this new movement.

Before finally taking up his quarters in St. Anne, Kankakee, State of Illinois, the seat of the chosen colony, he requested his official dismission from the diocese of Montreal, with which he had been connected for the five previous years. We give the answer in full, to show his standing when he left Canada for his new field.

[TRANSLATION.]

"MONTREAL, 13th October, 1851.

"SIR:—You ask me the permission to leave the diocese to go to offer your services to the Monseigneur of Chicago. As you belong to the diocese of Quebec, I believe that it appertains to Monseigneur, the Archbishop, to give you the *exeat* which you ask. For me, I cannot but thank you for your labors among us; and I wish you in return the most abundant blessings of Heaven. You shall ever be in my remembrance and in my heart; and I hope the Divine Providence will permit at a future time to testify to you all the gratitude that I feel within me. Meanwhile,

"I remain, dear sir,

"Your very humble and obedient servant,

"† IGNATIUS,
"*Bishop of Montreal*

"Mr. Chiniquy, Priest."

Thus he left Canada in the highest repute with the heirarchy of Rome. But a few years passed when the colony had expanded to the occupation of forty square miles, and thousands were still pouring in, not only from Canada, but from the Roman Catholic population of Europe. But in an evil day for Rome, Bishop Vandevelt was removed, and an Irish Bishop, O'Reagan, took his place and at once began to obstruct and oppress the French settlers. Here we state to Americans what is well known in Canada, that the French and Irish Roman Catholics seldom agree—there are violent feuds between them. The evidence, oppression and injustice of the Irish Bishop O'Reagan drove Father Chiniquy into resistance and to appeals to the outside Roman Catholic world for redress and deliverance from oppression. It came even to the Pope, and he sent Cardinal Bedeni to Chicago to investigate the dispute. He declared O'Reagan to be in the wrong, and he was removed, and Bishop Smith, of Iowa, took O'Reagan's place. While this storm was raging, God was opening the eyes of Father Chiniquy more and more to the real apostacy of the modern Papal Church from the old original Christian Church of Rome.

The hour of his deliverance was approaching, and God had chosen the field for the first fierce encounter under the liberty of the Stars and Stripes of the Republic of America. Anywhere else he would most likely be crushed to earth, but here he found freedom, and a noble-hearted advocate, when fiercely prosecuted, in the person of "honest" Abraham Lincoln, afterwards America's greatest President since the days of Washington.

To show that up to the time of his severance from Rome he bore the highest character, the following letter, from Bishop Baillargeon, of so late a date as 9th May, 1856, five years after he left Canada, amply proves.

[TRANSLATION.]

"ARCHBISHOP OF QUEBEC, 9th May, 1856.

"MISS:—I send you, for Mr. Chiniquy, an ornament [chasuble], with the necessary linen from which to make a cassock; and a chalice; the whole indifferently packed, as, I suppose, you will find a place for all in your trunk. And I pray God to bless you, and conduct you happily in your journey.

"Your devoted servant, C.J., *Bishop of Tloa.*"

"To Miss Caroline Descormers,
"*Of the Convent of the Ursulines of Three Rivers.*"

The Bishop sends by a nun of the Ursuline Convent of Three Rivers a present to Mr. Chiniquy, consisting of a chasuble, or the embroidered garment with a cross on the back, and a pillar in front, worn by priests; materials to make a cassock, and a chalice to perform Mass, as proofs of his highest confidence and esteem. Well would it be for the honor of the Church of Rome if she had many priests like him in the ranks of her clergy.

We now give the declaration of Bishop O'Reagan respecting Mr. Chiniquy's character, as sworn to by the four Roman Catholics whose names are appended. This written reply was given by Bishop O'Reagan on the 27th August, 1856, to the deputation who waited on him. This has been published all over Canada, in French and English, in reply to certain accusations of Vicar-General Bruyere:—

"1st. I suspended Mr. Chiniquy on the 19th of this month.

"2nd. If Mr. Chiniquy has said Mass since, as you say, he is irregular; and the Pope alone can restore him in his ecclesiastic and sacerdotal functions.

"3rd. I take him away from St. Anne, despite his prayers and yours, because he has not been willing to live in peace and in friendship with the Reverend M. L. and M. L., although I admit they were two bad Priests, whom I have been forced to expel from my diocese.

"4th. My second reason for taking Mr. Chiniquy away from St. Anne, to send him in his new mission, south of Illinois, is to stop the lawsuit Mr. Spink has instituted against him; though I cannot warrant that the law suit will be stopped for that.

"5th. **Mr.** Chiniquy is one of the best Priests of my diocese, and I do not want to deprive myself of his services; and no accusations against the morals of that gentleman have been proved before me.

"6th. **Mr.** Chiniquy has demanded an inquest, to prove his innocence of certain accusations made against him, and has asked me the names of his accusers to confound them; and I have refused it to him.

"7th. Tell Mr. Chiniquy to come and meet me—to prepare himself for his new mission, and I will give him the letters he needs, to go and labor there.

"Then we withdrew and presented the foregoing letter to Father Chiniquy.

FRS. BECHARD,
"J. B. LeMOINE,
"BASILIQUE ALLAIR,
"LEON MAILLOUX."

Nothing more can be wanted to establish the moral reputation of Mr. Chiniquy, so long as he remained in the Church of Rome.

DECLARATION

"Sir,—

"Since God has, in His infinite mercy, been pleased to show us the errors of Rome, and has given us strength to abandon them to follow Christ, we deem it our duty to say a word on the abominations of the confessional. You well know that these abominations are of such a nature that it is impossible for a woman to speak of them without a blush. How is it that among civilized, Christian men, one has so far forgotten the rule of common decency, as to force women to reveal to unmarried men, under the pains of eternal damnation, their most secret thoughts, their most sinful desires, and their most private actions?

"How, unless there be a brazen mask on your priest's face, dare they go out into the world having heard the tales of misery which cannot but defile the hearer, and which the woman cannot relate without having laid aside modesty, and all sense of shame? The harm would not be so great should the Church allow no one but the woman to accuse herself. But what shall we say of the abominable questions that are put to them and which they must answer?

"Here, the laws of common decency strictly forbid us to enter into details. Suffice it to say, were husbands cognizant of one-tenth of what is going on between the confessor and their wives, they would rather see them dead than degraded to such a degree.

"As for us, daughters and wives of Montreal, who have known by experience the filth of the confessional, we cannot sufficiently bless God for having shown us the error of our ways in teaching us that it is not at the feet of a man as weak and as sinful as ourselves, but at the feet of Christ alone, that we must seek salvation."

JULIEN HERBERT,
J. ROCHON,
FRANCOISE DIRINGER,
MARIE ROGERS,
LOUISE PICARD,
EUGENIE MARTIN,

And forty-three others.

PREFACE

EZEKIEL

CHAPTER VIII.

1. And it came to pass in the sixth year, in the sixth *month*, in the fifth *day* of the month, as I sat in mine house, and the elders of Judah sat before me, that the hand of the LORD GOD fell there upon me.

2. Then I beheld, and lo, a likeness as the appearance of fire; from the appearance of his loins even downward, fire; and from his loins even upward, as the appearance of brightness, as the color of amber.

3. And he put forth the form of an hand, and took me by a lock of mine head; and the spirit lifted me up between the earth and the heaven, and brought me in the visions of God to Jerusalem, to the door of the inner gate that looketh toward the north; where *was* the seat of the image of jealousy, which provoketh to jealousy.

4. And behold, the glory of the God of Israel *was* there, according to the vision that I saw in the plain.

5. ¶ Then said he unto me, Son of man, lift up thine eyes now the way toward the north. So I lifted up mine eyes the way toward the north; and behold, northward, at the gate of the altar, this image of jealousy in the entry.

6. He said furthermore unto me; Son of man, seest thou what they do? *even* the great abominations that the house of Israel committeth here, that I should go far off from my sanctuary? but turn thee yet again, *and* thou shalt see greater abominations.

7. ¶ And he brought me to the door of the court; and when I looked, behold, a hole in the wall.

8. Then said he unto me, Son of man, dig now in the wall: and when I had digged in the wall, behold, a door.

9. And he said unto me, Go in, and behold the wicked abominations that they do here.

10. So I went in and saw; and, behold, every form of creeping things, and abominable beasts, and all the idols of the house of Israel, portrayed upon the wall round about.

11. And there stood before them seventy men of the ancients of the house of Israel, and in the midst of them stood Jaazaniah the son of Shaphan, with every man his censer in his hand; and a thick cloud of incense went up.

12. Then said he unto me, Son of man, hast thou seen what the ancients of the house of Israel do in the dark, every man in the chambers of his imagery? for they say, The Lord seeth us not; the Lord hath forsaken the earth.

13. ¶ He said also unto me, Turn thee yet again, *and* thou shalt see greater abominations that they do.

14. Then he brought me to the door of the gate of the LORD'S house which *was* toward the north; and, behold, there sat women weeping for Tammuz.

15. ¶ Then said he unto me. Hast thou seen *this*, O Son of man? turn thee yet again, *and* thou shalt see greater abominations than these.

16. And he brought me into the inner court of the Lord's house, and, behold, at the door of the temple of the Lord, between the porch and the altar, were about five and twenty men, with their backs towards the temple of the Lord, and their faces toward the east; and they worshipped the sun toward the east.

17. ¶ Then he said unto me, Hast thou seen *this*, O Son of man? Is it a light thing to the house of Judah that they commit the abominations which they commit here? for they have filled the land with violence, and have returned to provoke me to anger; and, lo, they put the branch to their nose.

18. Therefore will I also deal in fury: mine eye shall not spare, neither will I have pity; and though they cry in mine ears with a loud voice, *yet* will I not hear them.

The Priest, the Woman, and the Confessional

CHAPTER I

THE STRUGGLE BEFORE THE SURRENDER OF WOMANLY SELF-RESPECT IN THE CONFESSIONAL

THERE are two women who ought to be constant objects of the compassion of the disciples of Christ, and for whom daily prayers ought to be offered at the mercy-seat—the Brahmin woman, who, deceived by her priests, burns herself on the corpse of her husband to appease the wrath of her wooden gods; and the Roman Catholic woman, who, not less deceived by her priests, suffers a torture far more cruel and ignominious in the confessional-box to appease the wrath of her wafer-god.

For I do not exaggerate when I say, that for many noble-hearted, well-educated, high-minded women, to be forced to unveil their hearts before the eyes of a man, to open to him all the most secret recesses of their souls, all the most sacred mysteries of their single or married life, to allow him to put to them questions which the most depraved woman would never consent to hear from her vilest seducer, is often more horrible and intolerable than to be tied on burning coals.

More than once, I have seen women fainting in the confessional-box, who told me afterwards, that the necessity of speaking to an unmarried man on certain things, on which the most common laws of decency ought to have for ever sealed their lips, had almost killed them! Not hundreds, but thousands of times, I have heard from the lips of dying girls, as well as of married women, the awful words; "I am forever lost! All my past confessions and communions have been so many sacrileges! Shame has sealed my lips and damned my soul!"

How many times I remained as one petrified, by the side of a corpse, when these last words having hardly escaped the lips of my female penitents, who had been snatched out of my reach by the merciless hand of death, before I could give her pardon through the deceitful sacramental absolution I then believed, as the dead sinner herself had believed, that she could not be forgiven except by that absolution.

For there are not only thousands but millions of Roman Catholic girls and women whose keen sense of modesty and womanly dignity are above all the sophisms and diabolical machinations of their priests. They never can be persuaded to answer "Yes" to certain questions of their confessors. They would prefer to be thrown into the flames, and burnt to ashes with the Brahmin widows, rather than allow the eyes of a man to pry into the sacred sanctuary of their souls. Though sometimes guilty before God, and under the impression that their sins will never be forgiven if not confessed, the laws of decency are stronger in their hearts than the laws of their cruel and perfidious Church. No consideration, not even the fear of eternal damnation, can persuade them to declare to a sinful man, sins which God alone has the right to know, for He alone can blot them out with the blood of His Son, shed on the cross.

But what a wretched life must that be of those exceptional noble souls, which Rome keeps in the dark dungeons of her superstition? They read in all their books, and hear from all their pulpits, that if they conceal a single sin from their confessors, they are forever lost! But, being absolutely unable to trample under their feet the laws of self-respect and decency, which God Himself has impressed in their souls, they live in constant dread of eternal damnation. No human words can tell their desolation and distress, when at the feet of their confessors, they find themselves under the horrible necessity of speaking of things, on which they would prefer to suffer the most cruel death rather than to open their lips, or to be forever damned if they do not degrade themselves forever in their own eyes, by speaking on matters which a respectable woman will never reveal to her own mother, much less to a man!

I have known only too many of these noble-hearted women, who, when alone with God, in a real agony of desolation and with burning tears, had asked Him to grant them what they considered the greatest favor, which was, to lose so much of their self-respect as to be enabled to speak of those unmentionable things, just as their confessors wanted them to speak; and, hoping that their petition had been granted, they went again to the confessional-box, determined to unveil their shame before the eyes of that inexorable man. But when the moment had come for the self-immolation, their courage failed, their knees trembled, their lips became pale as death, cold sweat poured from all their pores! The voice of modesty and womanly self-respect was speaking louder than the voice of their false religion. They had to go out of the confessional-box unpardoned—nay, with the burden of a new sacrilege on their conscience.

Oh! how heavy is the yoke of Rome—how bitter is human life —how cheerless is the mystery of the cross to those deluded and perishing souls! How gladly they would rush into the blazing piles with the Brahmin women, if they could hope to see the end of their unspeakable miseries through the momentary tortures which would open to them the gates of a better life!

I do hereby publicly challenge the whole Roman Catholic priesthood to deny that the greater part of the their female penitents remain a certain period of time—some longer, some shorter—under that most distressing state of mind.

Yes, by far the greater majority of women, at first, find it impossible to pull down the sacred barriers of self-respect which God Himself has built around their hearts, intelligences, and souls, as the best safeguard against the snares of this polluted world. Those laws of self-respect, by which they cannot consent to speak an impure word into the ears of a man, and which shut all the avenues of the heart against his unchaste questions, even when speaking in the name of God—those laws of self-respect are so clearly written in their conscience, and they are so well understood by them, to be a most Divine gift, that, as I have already said, many prefer to run the risk of being forever lost by remaining silent.

It takes many years of the most ingenious (I do not hesitate to call it diabolical) efforts on the part of the priests to persuade the majority of their female penitents to speak on questions, which even pagan savages would blush to mention among themselves. Some persist in remaining silent on those matters during the greater part of their lives, and many prefer to throw themselves into the hands of their merciful God, and die without submitting to the defiling ordeal, even after they have felt the poisonous stings of the enemy, rather than receive their pardon from a man, who, as they feel, would have surely been scandalized by the recital of their human frailties. All the priests of Rome are aware of this natural disposition of their female penitents. There is not a single one—no, not a single one of their moral theologians, who does not warn the confessors against that stern and general determination of the girls and married women never to speak in the confessional on matters which may, more or less, deal with sins against the seventh commandment. Dens, Liguori, Debreyne, Bailly, &c.,—in a word, all the theologians of Rome— own that this is one of the greatest difficulties which the confessors have to contend with in the confessional-box.

Not a single Roman Catholic priest will dare to deny what I say on this matter; for they know that it would be easy for me to overwhelm them with such a crowd of testimonies that their grand imposture would forever be unmasked.

I intend, at some future day, if God spares me and gives me time for it, to make known some of the innumerable things which the Roman Catholic theologians and moralists have written on this question. It will form one of the most curious books ever written; and it will give unanswerable evidence of the fact that, instinctively, without consulting each other, and with an unanimity which is almost marvellous, the Roman Catholic women, guided by the honest instincts which God has given them, shrink from the snare put before them in the confessional box; and that everywhere they struggle to nerve themselves with a superhuman courage, against the torturer who is sent by the Pope, to finish their ruin and to make shipwreck of their souls. Everywhere woman feels that there are things which ought never to be told, as there are things which ought never to be done, in the presence of the God of holiness. She understands that, to recite the history of certain sins, even of thought, is not less shameful and criminal than to do them; she hears the voice of God whispering into her ears, "Is it not enough that thou has been guilty once, when alone in My presence, without adding to thine iniquity by allowing that man to know what should never have been revealed to him? Do you not feel that you make that man your accomplice, the very moment that you throw into his heart and soul the mire of your iniquities? He is as weak as you are; he is not less a sinner than yourself; what has tempted you will tempt him; what has made you weak will make him weak; what has polluted you will pollute him; what has thrown you down into the dust, will throw him into the dust. Is it not enough that My eyes had to look upon your iniquities? Must My ears, to-day, listen to your impure conversation with that man? Were that man as holy as My prophet David, may he not fall before the unchaste unveiling of the new Bathsheba? Were he as strong as Samson, may he not find in you his tempting Delilah? Were he as generous as Peter, may be not become a traitor at the maidservant's voice?"

Perhaps the world has never seen a more terrible, desperate, solemn struggle than the one which is going on in the soul of a poor trembling young woman, who, at the feet of that man, has to decide whether or not she will open her lips on those things which the infallible voice of God, united to the no less infallible voice of her womanly honor and self-respect, tell her never to reveal to any man!

The history of that secret, fierce, desperate, and deadly struggle has never yet, so far as I know, been fully given. It would draw the tears of admiration and compassion of the whole world, if it could be written with its simple, sublime, and terrible realities.

How many times have I wept as a child when some noble-hearted and intelligent young girl, or some respectable married woman, yielding to the sophisms with which I, or some other confessor, had persuaded them to give up their self-respect, and their womanly dignity, to speak with me on matters on which a decent woman would never say a word with a man. They have told me of their invincible repugnance, their horror of such questions and answers, and they have asked me to have pity on them. Yes! I have often wept bitterly on my degradation, when a priest of Rome! I have realized all the strength, the grandeur, and the holiness of their motives for being silent on these defiling matters, and I could not but admire them. It seemed at times that they were speaking the language of angels of light; that I ought to fall at their feet, and ask their pardon for having spoken to them of questions on which a man of honor ought never to converse with a woman whom he respects.

But alas! I had soon to reproach myself, and regret these short instances of my wavering faith in the infallible voice of my Church; I had soon to silence the voice of my conscience, which was telling me, "Is it not a shame that you, an unmarried man, dare to speak on these matters with a woman? Do you not blush to put such questions to a young girl? Where is your self-respect? Where is your fear of God? Do you not promote the ruin of that girl by forcing her to speak with a man on such matters?"

I was compelled by all the Popes, the moral theologians, and the Councils, of Rome, to believe that this warning voice of my merciful God was the voice of Satan; I had to believe in spite of my own conscience and intelligence, that it was good, nay, necessary, to put those polluting, damning questions. My infallible Church was mercilessly forcing me to oblige those poor, trembling weeping, desolate girls and women, to swim with me and all her priests in those waters of Sodom and Gomorrah, under the pretext that their self-will would be broken down, their fear of sin and humility increased, and that they would be purified by our absolutions.

With what supreme distress, disgust, and surprise, we see, to-day, a great part of the whole Episcopal Church of England struck by a plague which seems incurable, under the name of Puseyism, or Ritualism, and bringing again—more or less openly —in many places the diabolical and filthy auricular confession among the Protestants of England, Australia and America. The Episcopal Church is doomed to perish in that dark and stinking pool of Popery—auricular confession, if she does not find a prompt remedy to stop the plague brought by the disguised

Jesuits, who are at work everywhere, to poison and enslave her too unsuspecting daughters and sons.

In the beginning of my priesthood, I was not a little surprised and embarrassed to see a very accomplished and beautiful young lady, whom I used to meet almost every week at her father's house, entering the box of my confessional. She had been used to confess to another young priest of my acquaintance, and she was always looked upon as one of the most pious girls of the city. Though she had disguised herself as much as possible, in order that I might not know her, I felt sure that I was not mistaken— she was the amiable Mary * * *

Not being absolutely certain of the correctness of my impressions, I left her entirely under the hope that she was a perfect stranger to me. At the beginning she could hardly speak; her voice was suffocated by her sobs; and through the little apertures of the thin partition between her and me, I saw two streams of big tears trickling down her cheeks.

After much effort, she said: "Dear Father, I hope you do not know me, and that you will never try to know me. I am a desperately great sinner. Oh! I fear that I am lost! But if there is still a hope for me to be saved, for God's sake, do not rebuke me! Before I begin my confession, allow me to ask you not to pollute my ears by questions which our confessors are in the habit of putting to their female penitents; I have already been destroyed by those questions. Before I was seventeen years old, God knows that His angels are not more pure than I was; but the chaplain of the Nunnery where my parents had sent me for my education, though approaching old age, put to me, in the confessional, a question which at first I did not understand, but, unfortunately, he had put the same questions to one of my young class-mates, who made fun of them in my presence, and explained them to me; for she understood them too well. This first unchaste conversation of my life plunged my thoughts in a sea of iniquity, till then absolutely unknown to me; temptations of the most humiliating character assailed me for a week, day and night; after which, sins which I would blot out with my blood, if it were possible, overwhelmed my soul as with a deluge. But the joys of the sinner are short. Struck with terror at the thought of the judgments of God, after a few weeks of the most deplorable life, I determined to give up my sins and reconcile myself to God. Covered with shame and trembling from head to foot, I went to confess to my old confessor, whom I respected as a saint and cherished as a father. It seems to me that, with sincere tears of repentance, I confessed to him the greatest part of my sins, though I concealed one of them, through shame, and respect for my spiritual guide. But I did not conceal from him that the strange questions he had put to me at my last confession, were, with the natural corruption of my heart, the principal cause of my destruction.

"He spoke to me very kindly, encouraged me to fight against my bad inclinations, and, at first, gave me very kind and good advice. But when I thought he had finished speaking, and as I was preparing to leave the confessional-box, he put to me two new questions of such a polluting character that I fear neither the blood of Christ nor all the fires of hell will ever be able to blot them out from my memory. Those questions have achieved my ruin; they have stuck to my mind like two deadly arrows; they are day and night before my imagination; they fill my very arteries and veins with a deadly poison.

"It is true that, at first, they filled me with horror and disgust; but alas! I soon got so accustomed to them that they seemed to be incorporated with me, and as if becoming a second nature. Those thoughts have become a new source of innumerable criminal thoughts, desires and actions.

"A month later, we were obliged by the rules of our convent to go and confess; but by this time, I was so completely lost, that I no longer blushed at the idea of confessing my shameful sins to a man; it was the very contrary. I had a real, diabolical pleasure in the thought that I should have a long conversation with my confessor on those matters, and that he would ask me more of his strange questions.

"In fact, when I had told him everything without a blush, he began to interrogate me, and God knows what corrupting things fell from his lips into my poor criminal heart! Every one of his questions was thrilling my nerves, and filling me with the most shameful sensations. After an hour of this criminal tête-a-tête with my old confessor (for it was nothing else but a criminal tête-tête), I perceived that he was as depraved as I was myself. With some half-covered words, he made a criminal proposition, which I accepted with covered words also; and during more than a year, we have lived together on the most sinful intimacy. Though he was much older than I, I loved him in the most foolish way. When the course of my convent instruction was finished, my parents called me back to their home. I was really glad of that change of residence, for I was beginning to be tired of my criminal life. My hope was that, under the direction of a better confessor, I should reconcile myself to God and begin a Christian life.

"Unfortunately for me, my new confessor, who was very young, began also his interrogations. He soon fell in love with me, and I loved him in a most criminal way. I have done with him things which I hope you will never request me to reveal to you, for they are too monstrous to be repeated, even in the confessional, by a woman to a man.

"I do not say these things to take away the responsibilities of my iniquities with this young confessor from my shoulders, for I think I have been more criminal than he was. It is my firm conviction that he was a good and holy priest before he knew me; but the questions he put to me, and the answers I had to give him, melted his heart—I know it—just as boiling lead would melt the ice on which it flows.

"I know this is not such a detailed confession as our holy Church requires me to make, but I have thought it necessary for me to give you this short history of the life of the greatest and most miserable sinner who ever asked you to help her to come out from the tomb of her iniquities. This is the way I have lived this past few years. But last Sabbath, God, in his infinite mercy, looked down upon me. He inspired you to give us the Prodigal Son as a model of true conversion, and as the most marvellous proof of the infinite compassion of the dear Saviour for the sinner. I have wept day and night since that happy day, when I threw myself into the arms of my loving merciful Father. Even now, I can hardly speak, because my regret for my past iniquities, and my joy that I am allowed to bathe the feet of the Saviour with tears, are so great that my voice is as choked.

"You understand that I have forever given up my last confessor. I come to ask you to do me the favor to receive me among your penitents. Oh! do not reject nor rebuke me, for the dear Saviour's sake! Be not afraid to have at your side such a monster of iniquity! But before going further, I have two favors to ask from you. The first is, that you will never do anything to ascertain my name; the second is, that you will never put to me any of those questions by which so many penitents are lost and so many priests forever destroyed. Twice I have been lost by those questions. We come to our confessors that they may throw upon our guilty souls the pure waters which flow from heaven to purify us; but instead of that, with their unmentionable questions, they pour oil on the burning fires which are already raging in our poor sinful hearts. Oh! dear father, let me become your penitent, that you may help me to go and weep with Magdalene at the Saviour's feet! Do respect me, as He respected that true model of all the sinful, but repenting women! Did our Saviour put to her any questions? Did He extort from her the history of things which a sinful woman cannot say without forgetting the respect she owes to herself and to God! No! you told us not long ago, that the only thing our Saviour did was to look at her tears and her love. Well, please do that and you will save me!"

I was then a very young priest, and never had any words so sublime come to my ears in the confessional-box. Her tears and her sobs, mingled with the frank declaration of the most humiliating actions, had made such a profound impression upon me that I was, for some time, unable to speak. It came to my mind also that I might be mistaken about her identity, and that perhaps she was not the young lady that I had imagined. I could, then, easily grant her first request, which was to do nothing by which I could know her. The second part of her prayer was more embarrassing; for the theologians are very positive in ordering the confessors to question their penitents, particularly those of the female sex, in many circumstances.

I encouraged her in the best way I could to persevere in her good resolutions, by invoking the blessed Virgin Mary and St. Philomène, who was, then, the Sainte à la mode, just as Marie Alacoque is to-day, among the blind slaves of Rome. I told her that I would pray and think over the subject of her second request; and I asked her to come back in a week for my answer.

The very same day, I went to my own confessor, the Rev. Mr. Baillargeon, then curate of Quebec, and afterwards Archbishop of Canada. I told him the singular and unusual request she had made, that I should never put to her any of those questions suggested by the theologians, to insure the integrity of the confession. I did not conceal from him that I was much inclined to grant her that favor; for I repeated what I had already several times told him, that I was supremely disgusted with the infamous and polluting questions which the theologians forced us to put to our female penitents. I told him frankly that several old and young priests had already come to confess to me; and that, with the exception of two, they had told me that they could not put those questions and hear the answers they elicited, without falling into the most damnable sins.

My confessor seemed to be much perplexed about what he should answer. He asked me to come the next day, that he might review some of his theological books in the interval. The next day I took down in writing his answer, which I find in my old manuscripts, and I give it here in all its sad crudity:—

"Such cases of the destruction of female virtue by the questions of the confessors is an unavoidable evil. It cannot be helped; for such questions are absolutely necessary in the greater part of the cases with which we have to deal. Men generally confess their sins with so much sincerity that there is seldom any need for questioning them, except when they are very ignorant. But St Liguori, as well as our personal observation, tells us that the greatest part of girls and women, through a false and criminal shame, very seldom confess the sins they commit against purity. It requires the utmost charity in the confessors to prevent those unfortunate slaves of their secret passions from making sacrilegious confessions and communions. With the greatest prudence and zeal he must question them on those matters, beginning with the smallest sins, and going, little by little, as much as possible by imperceptible degrees, to the most criminal actions. As it seems evident that the penitent referred to in your questions of yesterday is unwilling to make a full and detailed confession of all her iniquities, you cannot promise to absolve her without assuring yourself by wise and prudent questions, that she had confessed everything.

"You must not be discouraged when, through the confessional or any other way, you learn the fall of priests into the common frailties of human nature with their penitents. Our Saviour knew very well that the occasions and temptations we have to encounter, in the confessions of girls and women, are so numerous, and sometimes so irresistable, that many would fall. But He has given them the Holy Virgin Mary, who constantly asks and obtains their pardon; He has given them the sacrament of penance, where they can receive their pardon as often as they ask for it. The vow of perfect chastity is a great honor and privilege; but we cannot conceal from ourselves that it puts on our shoulders a burden which many cannot carry forever. St. Liguori says that we must not rebuke the penitent priest who falls only once a month; and some other trustworthy theologians are still more charitable."

This answer was far from satisfying me. It seemed to me composed of soft soap principles. I went back with a heavy heart and an anxious mind; and God knows that I made many fervent prayers that this girl should never come again to give me her sad history. I was hardly twenty-six years old, full of youth and life. It seemed to me that the stings of a thousand wasps to my ears would not do me so much harm as the words of that dear beautiful, accomplished, but lost girl.

I do not mean to say that the revelations which she made, had, in any way, diminished my esteem and my respect for her. It was just the contrary. Her tears and her sobs, at my feet; her agonizing expressions of shame and regret; her noble words of protest against the disgusting and polluting interrogations of the confessors, had raised her very high in my mind. My sincere hope was that she would have a place in the kingdom of Christ with the Samaritan women, Mary Magdalene, and all the sinners, who have washed their robes in the blood of the Lamb.

At the appointed day, I was in my confessional, listening to the confession of a young man, when I saw Miss Mary entering the vestry, and coming directly to my confessional-box, where she knelt by me. Though she had, still more than at the first time, disguised herself behind a long, thick, black veil, I could not be mistaken; she was the very same amiable young lady in whose father's house I used to pass such pleasant and happy hours. I had often listened, with breathless attention, to her melodius voice, when she was giving us, accompanied by her piano, some of our beautiful Church hymns. Who could then see and hear her without almost worshipping her? The dignity of her steps, and her whole mien, when she advanced towards my confessional, entirely betrayed her and destroyed her incognito.

Oh! I would have given every drop of my blood in that solemn hour, that I might have been free to deal with her just as she had so eloquently requested me to do—to let her weep and cry at the feet of Jesus to her heart's content; Oh! if I had been free to take her by the hand, and silently show her the dying Saviour, that she might have bathed His feet with her tears, and spread the oil of her love on His head, without my saying anything else but "Go in peace; thy sins are forgiven."

But, there, in that confessional-box, I was not the servant of Christ, to follow His divine, saving words, and obey the dictates of my honest conscience. I was the slave of the Pope! I had to stifle the cry of my conscience, to ignore the inspirations of my God! There, my conscience had no right to speak; my intelligence was a dead thing! The theologians of the Pope, alone, had a right to be heard and obeyed! I was not there to save, but to destroy; for, under the pretext of purifying, the real mission of the confessor, often, if not always, in spite of himself, is to scandilize and damn the souls.

As soon as the young man who was making his confession at my left hand, had finished, I, without noise, turned myself towards her, and said, through the little aperture, "Are you ready to begin your confession?"

But she did not answer me. All that I could hear was: "Oh, my Jesus, have mercy upon me! I come to wash my soul in Thy blood; wilt Thou rebuke me?"

During several minutes she raised her hands and her eyes to heaven, and wept and prayed. It was evident that she had not the least idea that I was observing her; she thought the door of the little partition between her and me was shut. But my eyes were fixed upon her; my tears were flowing with her tears, and my ardent prayers were going to the feet of Jesus with her prayers. I would not have interrupted her for any consideration, in this, her sublime communion with her merciful Saviour.

But after a pretty long time, I made a little noise with my hand, and putting my lips near the opening of the partition which was between us, I said in a low voice, "Dear sister, are you ready to begin your confession?"

She turned her face a little towards me, and said with trembling voice, "Yes, dear father, I am ready."

But she then stopped again to weep and pray, though I could not hear what she said.

After some time of silent prayer, I said, "My dear, sister, if you are ready, please begin your confession." She then said, "My dear father, do you remember the prayers which I made to you, the other day? Can you allow me to confess my sins without forcing me to forget the respect that I owe to myself, to you, and to God, who hears us? And can you promise that you will not put to me any of those questions which have already done me such irreparable injury? I frankly declare to you that there are sins that I cannot reveal to anyone, except to Christ, because He is my God, and that He already knows them all. Let me weep and cry at His feet: can you not forgive me without adding to my iniquities by forcing me to say things that the tongue of a Christian woman cannot reveal to a man?"

"My dear sister," I answered, "were I free to follow the voice of my own feelings I would be only too happy to grant your request; but I am here only as the minister of our holy Church, and bound to obey her laws. Through her most holy Popes and theologians she tells me that I cannot forgive your sins, if you do not confess them all, just as you have committed them. The Church tells me also that you must give the details which may add to the malice or change the nature of your sins. I am also sorry to tell you that our most holy theologians make it a duty of the confessor to question the penitent on the sins which he has good reason to suspect have been voluntarily or involuntarily omitted."

With a piercing cry, she exclaimed, "Then, O my God, I am lost—forever lost!"

This cry fell upon me like a thunderbolt; but I was still more terror-stricken when, looking through the aperture, I saw she was fainting; I heard the noise of her body falling upon the floor, and of her head striking against the sides of the confessional-box.

Quick as lightning I ran to help her, took her in my arms, and called a couple of men who were at a little distance, to assist me in laying her on a bench. I washed her face with some cold water and vinegar. She was as pale as death, but her lips were moving, and she was saying something which nobody but I could understand—

"I am lost—lost forever!"

We took her home to her disconsolate family, where, during a month, she lingered between life and death. Her two first confessors came to visit her; but having asked every one to go out of the room, she politely, but absolutely, requested them to go away, and never come again. She asked me to visit her every day, "for," she said, "I have only a few more days to live. Help me to prepare myself for the solemn hour which will open to me the gates of eternity!"

Every day I visited her, and I prayed and I wept with her.

Many times, when alone, with tears I requested her to finish her confession; but, with a firmness which, then, seemed to be mysterious and inexplicable, she politely rebuked me.

One day, when alone with her, I was kneeling by the side of her bed to pray, I was unable to articulate a single word, because of the inexpressible anguish of my soul on her account. She asked me, "Dear father, why do you weep?"

I answered, "How can you put such a question to your murderer! I weep because I have killed you, dear friend."

This answer seemed to trouble her exceedingly. She was very weak that day. After she had wept and prayed in silence, she said, "Do not weep for me, but weep for so many priests who destroy their penitents in the confessional. I believe in the holiness of the sacrament of penance, since our holy Church has established it. But there is, somewhere, something exceedingly wrong in the confessional. Twice I have been destroyed, and I know many girls who have also been destroyed by the confessional. This is a secret, but will that secret be kept forever? I pity the poor priests the day that our fathers will know what becomes of the purity of their daughters in the hands of their confessors. Father would surely kill my two last confessors, if he could know how they have destroyed his poor child."

I could not answer except by weeping.

We remained silent for a long time; then she said, "It is true that I was not prepared for the rebuke you have given me, the other day, in the confessional; but you acted conscientiously as a good and honest priest. I know you must be bound by certain laws."

She then pressed my hand with her cold hand and said, "Weep not, dear father, because that sudden storm has wrecked my too fragile bark. This storm was to take me out from the bottomless sea of my iniquities to the shore where Jesus was waiting to receive and pardon me. The night after you brought me, half dead, here to father's house I had a dream. Oh, no! it was not a dream, it was a reality. My Jesus came to me; He was bleeding; His crown of thorns was on His head, the heavy cross was bruising his shoulders. He said to me, with a voice so sweet that no human tongue can imitate it, "I have seen thy tears, I have heard thy cries, and I know thy love for Me: thy sins are forgiven; take courage; in a few days thou shalt be with me!"

She had hardly finished her last word, when she fainted; and I feared lest she should die just then, when I was alone with her.

I called the family, who rushed into the room. The doctor was sent for. He found her so weak that he thought proper to allow one or two persons to remain in the room with me. He requested us not to speak at all: "For," said he, "the least emotion may kill her instantly; her disease is, in all probability, an aneurism of the aorta, the big vein which brings the blood to the heart; when it breaks, she will go as quick as lightning."

It was nearly ten at night when I left the house to go and take some rest. But it is not necessary to say that I passed a sleepless night. My dear Mary was there, pale, dying from the deadly blow which I had given her in the confessional. She was there, on her bed of death, her heart pierced with the dagger which my Church had put into my hand! and instead of rebuking, and cursing me for my savage, merciless fanaticism, she was blessing me! She was dying from a broken heart, and I was not allowed by my Church to give her a single word of consolation and hope, for she had not made her confession! I had mercilessly bruised that tender plant, and there was nothing in my hands to heal the wounds I had made!

It was very probable that she would die the next day, and I was forbidden to show her the crown of glory which Jesus has prepared in His kingdom for the repenting sinner!

My desolation was really unspeakable, and I think I would have been suffocated and have died that night, if the stream of tears which constantly flowed from my eyes had not been as a balm to my distressed heart.

How dark and long the hours of that night seemed to me!

Before the dawn of day, I arose to read my theologians again, and see if I could not find some one who would allow me to forgive the sins of that dear child, without forcing her to tell me everything she had done. But they seemed to me, more than ever, unanimously inexorable, and I put them back on the shelves of my library with a broken heart.

At nine A.M. the next day, I was by the bed of our dear sick Mary. I cannot sufficiently tell the joy I felt when the doctor and the whole family said to me, "She is much better; the rest of last night has wrought a marvellous change indeed."

With a really angelic smile she extended her hand towards me, that I might press it in mine; and she said, "I thought, last evening, that the dear Saviour would take me to Him, but He wants me, dear father, to give you a little more trouble; however, be patient, it cannot be long before the solemn hour of the appeal will ring. Will you please read me the history of the suffering and death of the beloved Saviour, which you read me the other day? It does me so much good to see how He has loved me, such a miserable sinner."

There was a calm and a solemnity in her words which struck me singularly, as well as all those who were there.

After I had finished reading, she exclaimed, "He has loved me so much that He died for my sins!" And she shut her eyes as if to meditate in silence, but there was a stream of big tears rolling down her cheeks.

I knelt down by her bed, with her family, to pray; but I could not utter a single word. The idea that this dear child was there, dying from the cruel fanaticisms of my theologians and my own cowardice in obeying them, was a mill-stone to my neck. It was killing me.

Oh! if by dying a thousand times, I could have added a single day to her life, with what pleasure I would have accepted those thousand deaths!

After we had silently prayed and wept by her bedside, she requested her mother to leave her alone with me.

When I saw myself alone, under the irresistible impression that this was her last day, I fell on my knees again, and with tears of the most sincere compassion for her soul, I requested her to shake off her shame and to obey our holy Church, which requires every one to confess their sins if they want to be forgiven.

She calmly, but with an air of dignity which no human words can express, said, "Is it true that, after the sin of Adam and Eve, God Himself made coats and skins, and clothed them, that they might not see each other's nakedness?"

"Yes," I said "that is what the Holy Scripture tell us."

"Well, then, how is it possible that our confessors dare to take away from us that holy, divine coat of modesty and self-respect? Has not Almighty God Himself made, with His own hands that coat of womanly modesty and self-respect that we might not be to you and to ourselves, a cause of shame and sin?"

I was really stunned by the beauty, simplicity, and sublimity of that comparison. I remained absolutely mute and confounded. Though it was demolishing all the traditions and doctrines of my Church, and pulverizing all my holy doctors and theologians, that noble answer found such an echo in my soul, that it seemed to me a sacrilege to try to touch it with my finger.

After a short time of silence, she continued, "Twice I have been destroyed by priests in the confessional. They took away from me that divine coat of modesty and self-respect which God gives to every human being who comes into this world, and twice I have become for those very priests a deep pit of perdition, into which they have fallen, and where, I fear, they are forever lost! My merciful heavenly Father has given me back that coat of skins, that nuptial robe of modesty, self-respect, and holiness, which had been taken away from me. He cannot allow you or any other man, to tear again and spoil that vestment which is the work of His hands."

These words had exhausted her; it was evident to me that she wanted some rest. I left her alone, but I was absolutely beside myself. Filled with admiration for the sublime lessons which I had received from the lips of that regenerated daughter of Eve, who, it was evident, was soon to fly away from us, I felt a supreme disgust for myself, my theologians, and—shall I say it? yes, I felt in that solemn hour a supreme disgust for my Church, which was so cruelly defiling me, and all her priests in the confessional-box. I felt, in that hour, a supreme horror for that auricular confession, which is so often a pit of perdition and supreme misery for the confessor and penitent. I went out and walked two hours on the Plains of Abraham, to breathe the pure and refreshing air of the mountain. There, alone, I sat on a stone, on the very spot where Wolfe and Montcalm had fought and died; and I wept to my heart's content, on my irreparable degradation, and the degradation of so many priests through the confessional.

At four o'clock in the afternoon I went back again to the house of my dear dying Mary. The mother took me apart, and very politely said, "My dear Mr. Chiniquy, do you not think it is time that our dear child should receive the last sacraments? She seemed to be much better this morning, and we were full of hope; but she is now rapidly sinking. Please lose no time in giving her the holy viaticum and the extreme unction."

I said, "Yes, madam: let me pass a few minutes alone with our poor dear child, that I may prepare her for the last sacraments."

When alone with her, I again fell on my knees, and, amidst torrents of tears, I said, "Dear sister, it is my desire to give you the holy viaticum and the extreme unction; but tell me, how can I dare to do a thing so solemn against all the prohibitions of our Holy Church? How can I give you the holy communion without first giving you absolution? and how can I give you absolution when you earnestly persist in telling me that you have many sins which you will never declare either to me or any other confessor?

"You know that I cherish and respect you as if you were an angel sent to me from heaven. You told me, the other day, that you blessed the day that you first saw and knew me. I say the same thing. I bless the day that I have known you; I bless every hour that I have spent by your bed of suffering; I bless every tear which I have shed with you on your sins and on my own; I bless every hour we have passed together in looking to the wounds of our beloved, dying Saviour; I bless you for having forgiven me your death; for I know it, and I confess it in the presence of God, I have killed you, dear sister. But now I prefer a thousand times to die than to say to you a word which would pain you in any way, or trouble the peace of your soul. Please, my dear sister, tell me what I can and must do for you in this solemn hour."

Calmly, and with a smile of joy such as I had never seen before, nor seen since, she said, "I thank and bless you, dear father, for the parable of the Prodigal Son, on which you preached a month ago. You have brought me to the feet of the dear Saviour; there I have found a peace and a joy surpassing anything the human heart can feel; I have thrown myself into the arms of my Heavenly Father, and I know He has mercifully accepted and forgiven His poor prodigal child! Oh, I see the angels with their golden harps around the throne of the Lamb! Do you not hear the celestial harmony of their songs? I go—I go to join them in my Father's house. I SHALL NOT BE LOST!"

While she was thus speaking to me, my eyes were really turned into two fountains of tears; I was unable, as well as unwilling, to see anything, so entirely overcome was I by the sublime words which were flowing from the dying lips of that dear child, who was no more a sinner, but a real angel of Heaven to me. I was listening to her words; there was a celestial music in every one of them. But she had raised her voice in such a strange way, when she had begun to say, "I go to my Father's house," and she had made such a cry of joy when she had let the last words, "not be lost," escape her lips, that I raised my head and opened my eyes to look at her. I suspected that something strange had occurred.

I got upon my feet, passed my handkerchief over my face

to wipe away the tears which were preventing me from seeing with accuracy, and looked at her.

Her hands were crossed on her breast, and there was on her face the expression of a really super-human joy; her beautiful eyes were fixed as if they were looking on some grand and sublime spectacle; it seemed to me, at first, that she was praying.

In that very instant the mother rushed into the room, crying, "My God! my God! what does that cry 'lost' mean?"—For her last words, "not to be lost," particularly the last one, had been pronounced with such a powerful voice, that they had been heard almost everywhere in the house.

I made a sign with my hand to prevent the distressed mother from making any noise and troubling her dying child in her prayer, for I really thought that she had stopped speaking, as she used so often to do, when alone with me, in order to pray. But I was mistaken. That redeemed soul had gone, on the golden wings of love, to join the multitude of those who have washed their robes in the blood of the Lamb, to sing the eternal Alleluia.

CHAPTER II

IT WAS some time after our dear Mary had been buried. The terrible and mysterious cause of her death was known only to God and to myself. Though her loving mother was still weeping over her grave, as usual, she had soon been forgotten by the greatest part of those who had known her; but she was constantly present to my mind. I never entered the confessional-box without hearing her solemn, though so mild voice, telling me, "There must be, somewhere, something wrong in the auricular confession. Twice I have been destroyed by my confessors; and I have known several others who have been destroyed in the same way."

More than once, when her voice was ringing in my ears from her tomb, I had shed bitter tears on the profound and unfathomable degradation into which I, with the other priests, had to fall in the confessional-box. For many, many times, stories as deplorable as that of this unfortunate girl were confessed to me by city, as well as country females.

One night I was awakened by the rumbling noise of thunder, when I heard some one knocking at the door. I hastened out of bed to ask who was there. The answer was that the Rev. Mr. —— was dying, and that he wanted to see me before his death. I dressed myself, and was soon on the highway. The darkness was fearful; and often, had it not been for the lightning which was almost constantly tearing the clouds, we should not have known where we were. After a long and hard journey through the darkness and the storm, we arrived at the house of the dying priest. I went directly to his room, and really found him very low: he could hardly speak. With a sign of his hand he bade his servant girl, and a young man who were there, to go out, and leave him alone with me.

Then he said, in a low voice, "Was it you who prepared poor Mary to die?"

"Yes, sir," I answered.

"Please tell me the truth. Is it a fact that she died the death of a reprobate, and that her last words were, 'Oh, my God! I am lost!' "

I answered him, "As I was the confessor of that girl, and we were talking together on matters which pertained to her confession at the very moment that she was unexpectedly summoned to appear before God, I cannot answer your question in any way; please, then, excuse me if I cannot say any more on that subject: but tell me who can have assured you that she died the death of a reprobate!"

"It was her own mother," answered the dying man. "Last week she came to visit me, and when she was alone with me, with many tears and cries, she said how her poor child had refused to receive the last sacraments, and how her last cry was, 'I am lost!" She added that that cry, 'Lost!' was pronounced with such a frightful power that it was heard through all the house."

"If her mother told you that," I replied, "you may believe what you please about the way that poor child died. I cannot say a word—you know it—about the matter."

"But if she is lost," rejoined the old, dying priest, "I am the miserable one who has destroyed her. She was an angel of purity when she came to the convent. Oh! dear Mary, if you are lost, I am a thousandfold more lost! Oh, my God, my God! what will become of me? I am dying; and I am lost!"

It was indeed an awful thing to see that old sinner wringing his hands, and rolling on his bed, as if he had been on burning coals, with all the marks of the most frightful despair on his face, crying, "I am lost! Oh, my God, I am lost!"

I was glad that the claps of thunder which were shaking the house, and roaring without ceasing, prevented the people outside the room from hearing the cries of desolation from the priest, whom every one considered a great saint.

When it seemed to me his terror had somewhat subsided, and that his mind was calmed a little, I said to him, "My dear friend, you must not give yourself up to such despair. Our merciful God has promised to forgive the repenting sinner who comes to Him, even at the last hour of the day. Address yourself to the Virgin Mary, she will ask and obtain your pardon."

"Do you not think that it is too late to ask pardon? The doctor has honestly warned me that death is very near, and I feel that I am just now dying. Is it not too late to ask and obtain pardon?" asked the dying priest.

"No! my dear sir, it is not too late, if you sincerely regret your sins. Throw yourself into the arms of Jesus, Mary, and Joseph; make your confession without any more delay; I will absolve you, and you will be saved."

"But I have never made a good confession. Will you help me to make a general one?"

It was my duty to grant him his request, and the rest of the night was spent by me in hearing the confession of his whole life.

I do not want to give many particulars of the life of that priest. First: It was then that I understood why poor Mary was absolutely unwilling to mention the iniquities which she had committed with him. They were simply surpassingly horrible—unmentionable. No human tongue can express them—few human ears would consent to hear them.

The second thing that I am bound in conscience to reveal is almost incredible, but it is nevertheless true. The number of married and unmarried females he had heard in the confessional was about 1,500, of whom he said he had destroyed or scandalised at least 1,000 by his questioning them on most depraved things, for the simple pleasure of gratifying his own corrupted heart, without letting them know anything of his sinful thoughts and criminal desires towards them. But he confessed that he had destroyed the purity of ninety-five of those penitents, who had consented to sin with him.

And would to God that this priest had been the only one whom I have known to be lost through the auricular confession. But, alas! how few are those who have escaped the snares of the tempter compared with those who have perished? I have heard the confessions of more than 200 priests, and to say the truth, as God knows it, I must declare that only twenty-one had not to weep over the secret or public sins committed through the irresistibly corrupting influences of auricular confession!

I am now more than seventy-seven years old, and in a short time I shall be in my grave. I shall have to give an account of what I now say. Well, it is in the presence of my great Judge, with my tomb before my eyes, that I declare to the world that very few—yes, very few—priests escape from falling into the pit of the most horrible moral depravity the world has ever known, through the confession of females.

I do not say this because I have any bad feelings against those priests; God knows I have none. The only feelings I have are of supreme compassion and pity. I do not reveal these awful things to make the world believe that the priests of Rome are a worse set of men than the rest of the innumerable fallen children of Adam; no; I do not entertain any such views; for everything considered, and weighed in the balance of religion, charity and common sense—I think that the priests of Rome are far from being worse than any other set of men who would be thrown into the same temptations, dangers, and unavoidable occasions of sin.

For instance, let us take lawyers, merchants, or farmers, and, preventing them from living with their lawful wives, let us surround each of them from morning to night, by ten, twenty, and sometimes more, beautiful women and tempting girls, who would speak to them of things which would pulverize a rock of Scotch granite, and you will see how many of those lawyers, merchants, or farmers would come out of that terrible moral battle-field without being mortally wounded.

The cause of the supreme—I dare say incredible, though unsuspected—immorality of the priests of Rome is a very evident and logical one. By the diabolical power of the Pope, the priest is put out of the ways which God has offered to the generality of men to be honest, upright and holy.* And after the Pope has deprived them of the grand, holy, and Divine (in this sense that it comes directly from God) remedy which God has given to man against his own concupiscence—holy marriage, they are placed unprotected and unguarded in the most perilous, difficult, and irresistible moral dangers which human ingenuity or depravity can conceive. Those unmarried men are forced, from morning to night, to be in the midst of beautiful girls, and tempting, charming women, who have to tell them things which would melt the hardest steel. How can you expect that they will cease to be men, and become stronger than angels?

Not only are the priests of Rome deprived by the devil of the only remedy which God has given to help them to withstand, but in the confessional they have the greatest facility which can possibly be imagined for satisfying all the bad propensities of fallen human nature. In the confessional they know those who are strong, and they also know those who are weak among the females by whom they are surrounded; they know who would resist any attempt from the enemy; and they know who are ready—nay, who are longing after the deceitful charms of sin. If they still retain the fallen nature of man, what a terrible hour for them? what frightful battles inside the poor heart? what superhuman effort and strength would be required to come out a conqueror from the battle-field, where a David and a Samson have fallen mortally wounded?

It is simply an act of supreme stupidity on the part of the Protestant, as well as Catholic public, to suppose, or suspect, or hope that the generality of the priests can stand such a trial. The pages of the history of Rome herself are filled with unanswerable proofs that the great generality of the confessors fall. If it were not so, the miracle of Joshua, stopping the march of the sun and the moon, would be childish play compared with the miracle which would stop and reverse all the laws of our common fallen nature in the hearts of the 100,000 Roman Catholic confessors of the Church of Rome. Were I attempting to

---

* "To avoid fornication, let every man have his own wife, and let every woman have her own husband." (i Cor. vii, 2.)

prove, by public facts, what I know of the horrible depravity caused by the confessional-box among the priests of France, Canada, Spain, Italy, and England, I should have to write many big volumes in folio. For brevity's sake, I will speak only of Italy. I take that country, because, being under the very eyes of their infallible and most holy (?) pontiff, being in the land of daily miracles, of painted Madonnas, who weep and turn their eyes left and right, up and down, in a most marvellous way, being in the land of miraculous medals and heavenly spiritual favors, constantly flowing from the chair of St. Peter, the confessors in Italy, seeing every year the miraculous melting of the blood of St. January, having in their midst the hair of the Virgin Mary, and a part of her shirt, are in the best possible circumstances to be strong, faithful and holy. Well, let us hear the testimony of an eye-witness, a contemporary, and an unimpeachable witness about the way the confessors deal with the penitent females in the holy, apostolical, infallible (?) Church of Rome.

The witness we will hear is of the purest blood of the princes of Italy. Her name is Henrietta Carracciolo, daughter of the Marshal Carracciolo, Governor of the Province of Pari, in Italy. Let us hear what she says of the Father Confessors, after twenty years of personal experience in different nunneries of Italy, in her remarkable book, "Mysteries of the Neapolitan Convents," pp. 150, 151, 152: "My confessor came the following day, and I disclosed to him the nature of the troubles which beset me. Later in the day, seeing that I had gone down to the place where we used to receive the holy communion, called Communichino, the conversa of my aunt rang the bell for the priest to come with the pyx.* He was a man of about fifty years of age, very corpulent, with a rubicund face, and a type of physiognomy as vulgar as it was repulsive.

"I approached the little window to receive the sacred wafer on my tongue, with my eyes closed, as is customary. I placed it on my tongue, and, as I drew back, I felt my cheeks caressed. I opened my eyes, but the priest had withdrawn his hand, and, thinking I had been deceived, I gave it no more attention.

"On the next occasion, forgetful of what had occurred before, I received the sacrament with closed eyes again, according to precept. This time I distinctly felt my chin caressed again, and on opening my eyes suddenly, I found the priest gazing rudely upon me with a sensual smile on his face.

"There could be no longer any doubt; these overtures were not the result of accident.

---

* A silver box containing consecrated bread, which is believed to be the real body, blood and divinity of Jesus Christ.

"The daughter of Eve is endowed with a greater degree of curiosity than man. It occurred to me to place myself in a contiguous apartment, where I could observe whether this libertine priest was accustomed to take similar liberties with the nuns. I did so, and was fully convinced that only the old left him without being caressed.

"All the others allowed him to do with them as he pleased; and even, in taking leave of him, did so with the utmost reverence.

" 'Is this the respect,' said I to myself, 'that the priests and the spouses of Christ have for their sacrament of the Eucharist? Shall the poor novice be enticed to leave the world in order to learn, in this school, such lessons of self-respect and chastity?' "

Page 163, we read: "The fanatical passion of the nuns for their confessors, priests, and monks, exceeds belief. That which especially renders their incarceration endurable is the illimitable opportunity they enjoy of seeing and corresponding with those persons with whom they are in love. This freedom localizes and identifies them with the convent so closely that they are unhappy, when, on account of any serious sickness, or while preparing to take the veil, they are obliged to pass some months in the bosom of their own families, in company with their fathers, mothers, brothers, and sisters. It is not to be presumed that these relatives would permit a young girl to pass many hours, each day, in a mysterious colloquy with a priest, or a monk, and maintain with him this correspondence. This is a liberty which they can enjoy in the convent only.

"Many are the hours which the Heloise spends in the confessional, in agreeable pastime with her Abelard in cassock.

"Others, whose confessors happen to be old, have in addition a spiritual director, with whom they amuse themselves a long time every day téte-a-téte, in the parlatoria. When this is not enough, they simulate an illness, in order to have him alone in their own rooms."

Page 166, we read: "Another nun, being somewhat infirm, her priest confessed her in her room. After a time, the invalid penitent found herself in what is called an interesting situation, on which account, the physician declaring that her complaint was dropsy, she was sent away from the convent."

Page 167: "A young educanda was in the habit of going down every night, to the convent burying-place, where, by a corridor which communicated with the vestry, she entered into a colloquy with a young priest attached to the church. Consumed by an amorous passion, she was not deterred by bad weather or the fear of being discovered.

"She heard a great noise, one night, near her. In the thick darkness which surrounded her, she imagined that she saw a viper winding itself round her feet. She was so much overcome by fright, that she died from the effects of it a few months later."

Page 168: "One of the confessors had a young penitent in the convent. Every time he was called to visit a dying sister, and on that account passed the night in the convent, this nun would climb over the partition which separated her room from his, and betake herself to the master and director of her soul.

"Another, during the delirium of a typhoid fever from which she was suffering, was constantly imitating the action of sending kisses to her confessor, who stood by the side of her bed. He, covered with blushes on account of the presence of strangers, held a crucifix before the eyes of the penitent, and exclaimed in a commiserating tone:—

" 'Poor thing! kiss thy own spouse!' "

Page 168: "Under the bonds of secresy, an educanda, of fine form and pleasing manners, and of a noble family, confided to me the fact of her having received, from the hands of her confessor, a very interesting book (as she described it) which related to the monastic life. I expressed the wish to know the title, and she, before showing it to me, took the precaution to lock the door.

"It proved to be the Monaca, by Dalembert, a book as all know, filled with the most disgusting obscenity."

Page 169: "I received once, from a monk, a letter in which he signified to me that he had hardly seen me when 'he conceived the sweet hope of becoming my confessor.' An exquisite of the first water, a fop of scents and euphuism, could not have employed phrases more melodramatic, to demand whether he might hope or despair."

Page 169: "A priest who enjoyed the reputation of being an incorruptible sacerdote, when he saw me pass through the parlatoria, used to address me as follows:—

" 'Ps, dear, come here; Ps, Ps, come here!'

"These words, addressed to me by a priest, were nauseous in the extreme.

"Finally, another priest, the most annoying of all for his obstinate assiduity, sought to secure my affections at all cost. There was not an image profane poetry could afford him, nor a sophism he could borrow from rhetoric, nor wily interpretation he could give to the Word of God, which he did not employ to convert me to his wishes. Here is an example of his logic:—

" 'Fair daughter,' said he to me one day, knowest thou who God truly is?'

" 'He is the Creator of the Universe,' I answered drily.

" 'No,—no,—no,—no! that it is not enough,' he replied, laughing at my ignorance. 'God is love, but love in the abstract, which receives its incarnation in the mutual affection of two hearts which idolise each other. You, then, must not only love God in His abstract existence, but must also love Him in His incarnation, that is, in the exclusive love of a man who adores you. Quod Deus est amor, nec colitur nisi amando.'

" 'Then,' I replied, 'a woman who adores her own lover would adore Divinity itself?'

" 'Assuredly,' reiterated the priest, over and over again, taking courage from my remark, and chuckling at what seemed to him to be the effect of his catechism.

" 'In that case,' said I, hastily, "I should select for my lover rather a man of the world than a priest.'

" 'God preserve you, my daughter! God preserve you from that sin!' added my interlocutor, apparently frightened, 'To love a man of the world, a sinner, a wretch, an unbeliever, an infidel! Why, you would go immediately to hell. The love of a priest is a sacred love, while that of a profane man is infamy; the faith of a priest emanates from that granted to the holy Church, while that of the profane is false—false as the vanity of the world. The priest purifies his affections daily in communion with the Holy Spirit; the man of the world (if he ever knows love at all) sweeps the muddy crossings of the street with it day and night.'

" 'But it is the heart, as well as the conscience, which prompts me to fly from the priests,' I replied.

" 'Well, if you cannot love me because I am your confessor, I will find means to assist you to get rid of your scruples. We will place the name of Jesus Christ before all our affectionate demonstrations, and thus our love will be a grateful offering to the Lord, and will ascend fragrant with perfume to Heaven, like the smoke of the incense of the sanctuary. Say to me, for example, "I love you in Jesus Christ; last night I dreamed of you in Jesus Christ;" and you will have a tranquil conscience, because in doing this you will sanctify every transport of your love.'

"Several circumstances not indicated here, by the way, compelled me to come in frequent contact with this priest afterwards, and I do not, therefore, give his name.

"Of a very respectable monk, respectable alike for his age and his moral character, I enquired what signified the prefixing the name of Jesus Christ to amorous apostrophes.

" 'It is,' he said, 'an expression used by a horrible sect, and one unfortunately only too numerous, which, thus abusing the name of our Lord, permits to its members the most unbridled licentiousness.' "

And it is my sad duty to say, before the whole world, that I know that by far the greater part of the confessors in America, Spain, France, and England, reason and act just like that licentious Italian priest.

Christian nations! If you could know what will become of the virtue of your fair daughters if you allow secret or public slaves of Rome under the name of Ritualists to restore the auricular confession, with what a storm of holy indignation you would defeat their plans!

CHAPTER III

IF ANYONE wants to hear an eloquent oration, let him go where the Roman Catholic priest is preaching on the divine institution of auricular confession. There is no subject, perhaps, on which the priests display so much zeal and earnestness, and of which they speak so often. For this institution is really the corner-stone of their stupendous power; it is the secret of their irresistible influence. Let the people open their eyes, to-day, to the truth, and understand that auricular confession is one of the most stupendous impostures which Satan has invented, to corrupt and enslave the world; let the people desert the confessional-box to-day, and to-morrow Romanism will fall into the dust. The priests understand this very well; hence their constant efforts to deceive the people on that question. To attain their object, they have recourse to the most egregious falsehoods; the Scriptures are misrepresented; the holy Fathers are brought to say the very contrary of what they have ever thought or written; and the most extraordinary miracles and stories are invented. But two of the arguments to which they have more often recourse, are the great and perpetual miracles which God makes to keep the purity of the confessional undefiled, and its secrets marvellously sealed. They make the people believe that the vow of perpetual chastity changes their nature, turns them into angels, and puts them above the common frailties of the fallen children of Adam.

Bravely, and with a brazen face, when they are interrogated on that subject, they say that they have special graces to remain pure and undefiled in the midst of the greatest dangers; that the Virgin Mary, to whom they are consecrated, is their powerful advocate to obtain from her Son that superhuman virtue of chastity; that what would be a cause of sure perdition to commen men, is without peril and danger for a true Son of Mary; and, with amazing stupidity, the people consent to be duped, blinded, and deceived by those fooleries.

But here, let the world learn the truth as it is, from one who knows perfectly everything inside and outside the walls of that Modern Babylon. Though many, I know, will disbelieve me and say, "We hope you are mistaken; it is impossible that the priests of Rome should turn out to be such impostors; they may be mistaken; they may believe and repeat things which are not true, but they are honest; they cannot be such impudent deceivers."

Yes; though I know that many will hardly believe me, I must tell the truth.

Those very men, who, when speaking to the people in such

glowing terms of the marvellous way they are kept pure, in the midst of the dangers which surround them, honestly blush—and often weep—when they speak to each other (when they are sure that nobody, except priests, hear them). They deplore their own moral degradation with the utmost sincerity and honesty; they ask from God and men, pardon for their unspeakable depravity.

I have here—in my hands, and under my eyes—one of their most remarkable secret books, written (or at least approved) by one of their greatest and best bishops and cardinals, the Cardinal de Bonald, Archbishop of Lyons.

The book is written for the use of priests alone. Its title is, in French, "Examen de Conscience des Prêtres." At page 34, we read:

"Have I left certain persons to make the declarations of their sins in such a way that the imagination, once taken and impressed by pictures and representations, could be dragged into a long course of temptations and grevious sins? The priests do not pay sufficient attention to the continual temptations caused by the hearing of confessions. The soul is gradually enfeebled in such a way that, at the end, the virtue of chastity is forever lost."

Here is the address of a priest to other priests, when he suspects that nobody but his co-sinner brethren hear him. Here is the honest language of truth.

In the presence of God those priests acknowledge that they have not a sufficient fear of those constant (what a word—what an acknowledgment—constant!) temptations, and they honestly confess that these temptations come from the hearing of the confessions of so many scandalous sins. Here the priests honestly acknowledge that those constant temptations, at the end, destroy forever in them the holy virtue of purity.*

Ah! would to God that all the honest girls and women whom the devil entraps into the snares of auricular confession, could hear the cries of distress of those poor priests whom they have tempted—forever destroyed! Would to God that they could see the torrents of tears shed by so many priests, because, from the hearing of confessions, they had forever lost the virtue of purity! They would understand that the confessional is a snare, a pit of perdition, a Sodom for the priest; and they would be struck with horror and shame at the idea of the continual, shameful, dishonest, degrading temptations, by which their confessor is tormented day and night—they would blush on account of the shameful sins which their confessors have committed— they would weep over the irreparable loss of their purity—they

* And remark, that all their religious authors who have written on that subject hold the same language. They all speak of those continual degrading temptations; they all lament the damning sins which follow those temptations; they all entreat the priests to fight those temptations and repent of those sins.

would promise before God and men that the confessional-box should never see them any more—they would prefer to be burned alive, if any sentiment of honesty and charity remained in them, rather than consent to be a cause of constant temptations and damnable sins to that man.

Would that respectable lady go any more to confess to that man, if, after her confession, she could hear him lamenting the continual, shameful temptations which assail him day and night, and the damning sins which he has committed on account of what she has confessed to him? No?—a thousand times, no!

Would that honest father allow his beloved daughter to go any more to that man to confess, if he could hear his cries of distress, and see his tears flowing, because the hearing of those confessions is the source of constant, shameful temptations and degrading iniquities?

Oh! I would to God that the honest Romanists all over the world—for there are millions, who, though deluded, are honest —could see what is going on in the heart, and the imagination of the poor confessor when he is, there, surrounded by attractive women and tempting girls, speaking to him from morning to night on things which a man cannot hear without falling. Then, that modern but grand imposture, called the Sacrament of Penance, would soon be ended.

But here, again, who will not lament the consequences of the total perversity of human nature? Those very same priests who, when alone, in the presence of God, speak so plainly of the constant temptations by which they are assailed, and who so sincerely weep over the irreparable loss of their virture of purity, when they think that nobody hears them, will yet, in public, with a brazen face, deny those temptations. They will indignantly rebuke you as a slanderer if you say anything to lead them to suppose that you fear for their purity, when they hear the confessions of girls or married women!

There is not a single one of the Roman Catholic authors, who have written on that subject for the priests, who has not deplored their innumerable and degrading sins against purity, on account of the auricular confession; but those very men will be the first to try to prove the very contrary when they write books for the people. I have no words to tell what was my surprise when, for the first time, I saw that this strange duplicity seemed to be one of the fundamental stones of my Church.

It was not very long after my ordination, when a priest came to me to confess the most deplorable things. He honestly told me that there was not a single one of the girls or married women whom he had confessed, who had not been a secret cause of the most shameful sins, in thought, desires, or actions; but he wept so bitterly over his degradation, his heart seemed so sincerely broken on account of his own iniquities, that I could not refrain from mixing my tears with his; I wept with him, and I gave him pardon for all his sins, as I then thought I had the power and right to give it.

Two hours afterwards, that same priest, who was a good speaker, was in the pulpit. His sermon was on "The Divinity of Auricular Confession;" and, to prove that it was an institution coming directly from Christ, he said that the Son of God was performing a constant miracle to strengthen His priests, and prevent them from falling into sins, on account of what they might have heard in the confessional!!!

The daily abominations, which are the result of auricular confession, are so horrible and so well known by the popes, the bishops, and the priests, that several times public attempts have been made to diminish them by punishing the guilty priests; but all these commendable efforts have failed.

One of the most remarkable of those efforts was made by Pius IV about the year 1560. A Bull was published by him, by which all the girls and married women who had been seduced into sins by their confessors, were ordered to denounce them; and a certain number of high church officers of the Holy Inquisition were authorized to take the depositions of the fallen penitents. The thing was, at first, tried at Seville, one of the principal cities of Spain. When the edict was first published, the number of women who felt bound in conscience to go and depose against their father confessors, was so great, that though there were thirty notaries, and as many inquisitors, to take the depositions, they were unable to do the work in the appointed time. Thirty days more were given, but the inquisitors were so overwhelmed with the numberless depositions, that another period of time of the same length was given. But this, again, was found insufficient. At the end, it was found that the number of priests who had destroyed the purity of their penitents was so great that it was impossible to punish them all. The inquest was given up, and the guilty confessors remained unpunished. Several attempts of the same nature have been tried by other popes, but with about the same success.

But if those honest attempts on the part of some well-meaning popes, to punish the confessors who destroy the purity of the penitents, have failed to touch the guilty parties, they are, in the good providence of God, infallible witnesses to tell to the world that auricular confession is nothing else than a snare to the confessor and his dupes. Yes, those Bulls of the popes are an irrefragable testimony that auricular confession is the most powerful invention of the devil to corrupt the heart, pollute the body, and damn the soul of the priest and his female penitent!

CHAPTER IV

A RE not facts the best arguments? Well, here is an undeniable, a public fact, which is connected with a thousand
collateral ones, to prove that auricular confession is the most
powerful machine of demoralization which the world has ever
seen.

About the year 1830, there was in Quebec a fine-looking
young priest; he had a magnificent voice, and was a pretty good
speaker.* Through regard for his family, which is still numerous and respectable, I will not give his name: I will call him
Rev. Mr. D——. Having been invited to preach in a parish of
Canada, about 100 miles distant from Quebec, called Vercheres,
he was also requested to hear the confessions, during a few days
of a kind of Novena (nine days of revival), which was going
on in that place. Among his penitents was a beautiful young girl,
about nineteen years old. She wanted to make a general confession of all her sins from the first age of reason, and the confessor
granted her request. Twice, every day, she was there, at the feet
of her handsome young spiritual physician, telling all her
thoughts, her deeds, and her desires. Sometimes she was re-
marked to have remained a whole hour in the confessional-box,
accusing herself of all her human frailties. What did she say?
God only knows; but what became hereafter known by a great
part of the entire part of the population of Canada is, that the
confessor fell in love with his fair penitent, and that she burned
with the same irresistible fires for her confessor—as it so often
happens.

It was not an easy matter for the priest and the young girl
to meet each other in as complete a tête-a-tête as they both
wished; for there were too many eyes upon them. But the confessor was a man of resources. On the last day of Novena, he
said to his beloved penitent, "I am going now to Montreal; but
in three days, I will take the steamer back to Quebec. That
steamer is accustomed to stop here. At about twelve, at night,
be on the wharf dressed as a young man; but let no one know
your secret. You will embark in the steamboat, where you will
not be known, if you have any prudence. You will come to Quebec,
where you will be engaged as a servant boy by the curate, of
whom I am the vicar. Nobody will know your sex except myself,
and, there, we will be happy together."

---

* He is dead long ago.

The fourth day after this, there was a great desolation in the family of the girl; for she had suddenly disappeared, and her robes had been found on the shores of the St. Lawrence River. There was not the least doubt in the minds of all relations and friends, that the general confession she had made had entirely upset her mind; and in an excess of craziness, she had thrown herself into the deep and rapid waters of the St. Lawrence. Many searches were made to find her body; but, of course, all in vain. Many public and private prayers were offered to God to help her escape from the flames of Purgatory, where she might be condemned to suffer for many years, and much money was given to the priest to sing high masses, in order to extinguish the fires of that burning prison, where every Roman Catholic believes he must go to be purified before entering the regions of eternal happiness.

I will not give the name of the girl, though I have it, through compassion for her family; I will call her Geneva.

Well, when father and mother, brothers, sisters, and friends were shedding tears at the sad end of Geneva, she was in the parsonage of the rich Curate of Quebec, well paid, well fed, and dressed—happy and cheerful with her beloved confessor. She was exceedingly neat in her person, always obliging, and ready to run and do what you wanted at the very twinkling of your eye. Her new name was Joseph, by which I will now call her.

Many times I have seen the smart Joseph at the parsonage of Quebec, and admired his politeness and good manners; though it seemed to me, sometimes, that he looked too much like a girl, and that he was a little too much at ease with the Rev. Mr. D——, and also with the Right Rev. Bishop M——. But every time the idea came to me that Joseph was a girl, I felt indignant with myself. The high respect I had to the Coadjutor Bishop, who was also the Curate of Quebec, made it almost impossible to imagine that he would ever allow a beautiful girl to sleep in the adjoining room to his own, and to serve him day and night; for Joseph's sleeping-room was just by that of the Coadjutor, who, for several bodily infirmities (which were not a secret to every one), wanted the help of his servant several times at night, as well as during the day.

Things went on very smoothly with Joseph during two or three years, in the Coadjutor Bishop's house; but at the end, it seemed to many people outside, that Joseph was taking too great airs of familiarity with the young vicars, and even with the venerable Coadjutor. Several of the citizens of Quebec, who were going more often than others to the parsonage, were surprised and shocked at the familiarity of that servant boy with his masters; he really seemed sometimes to be on equal terms with, if not somewhat above them.

An intimate friend of the Bishop—a most devoted Roman Catholic—who was my near relative, took upon himself one day to respectfully say to the Right Rev. Bishop that it would be prudent to turn out that impudent young man from his palace— that he was the object of strong and most deplorable suspicions.

The position of the Right Rev. Bishop and his vicars, was, then, not a very agreeable one. Their barque had evidently drifted among dangerous rocks. To keep Joseph among them was impossible, after the friendly advice which had come from such a high quarter; and to dismiss him was not less dangerous; he knew too much of the interior and secret lives of all these holy (?) celibates, to deal with him as with another common servant-man. With a single word of his lips he could destroy them: they were as if tied to his feet by ropes, which, at first, seemed made with sweet cakes and ice-cream, but had suddenly turned into burning steel chains. Several days of anxiety passed away, and many sleepless nights succeeded the too happy ones of better times. But what was to be done? There were breakers ahead; breakers on the right, on the left, and on every side. However, everyone, particularly the venerable (?) Coadjutor, felt as criminals who expect their sentence, and that their horizon seemed surrounded absolutely by only dark and stormy clouds, a happy opening suddenly presented itself to the anxious sailors.

The curate of "Les Eboulements," the Rev. Mr. Clement, had just come to Quebec on some private business, and had taken up his quarters in the hospitable house of his old friend, the Right Rev. ——, Bishop Coadjutor. Both had been on very intimate terms for many years, and in many instances they had been of great service to each other. The Pontiff of the Church of Canada, hoping that his tried friend would perhaps help him out of the terrible difficulty of the moment, frankly told him all about Joseph, and asked him what he ought to do under such difficult circumstances.

"My Lord," said the curate of the Eboulements, "Joseph is just the servant I want. Pay him well, that he may remain your friend, and that his lips may be sealed, and allow me to take him with me. My housekeeper left me a few weeks ago; I am alone in my parsonage with my old servant-man. Joseph is just the person I want."

It would be difficult to tell the joy of the poor Bishop and his vicars, when they saw that heavy stone they had on their neck thus removed.

Joseph, once installed into the parsonage of the pious (?) parish priest of the Eboulements, soon gained the favor of the whole people by his good and winning manners, and every parishioner complimented the curate on the smartness of his new servant. The priest, of course, knew a little more of that smartness than the rest of the people. Three years passed on very smoothly. The priest and his servant seemed to be on the most perfect terms. The only thing which marred the happiness of that lucky couple was that, now and then, some of the farmers whose eyes were sharper than those of their neighbors, seemed to think that the intimacy between the two was going a little too far, and that Joseph was really keeping in his hands the sceptre of the little priestly kingdom. Nothing could be done without his advice; he was meddling in all the small and big affairs of the parish, and the curate seemed sometimes to be rather the servant than the master in his own house and parish. Those who had, at first, made these remarks privately, began, little by little, to convey their views to their next neighbor, and this one to the next: in that way, at the end of the third year, grave and serious suspicions began to spread from one to the other in such a way that the Marguilliers (a kind of Elders), thought proper to say to the priest that it would be better for him to turn Joseph out than to keep him any longer. But the old curate had passed so many happy hours with his faithful Joseph that it was as hard as death to give him up.

He knew, by confession, that a girl in the vicinity was given to an unmentionable abomination, to which Joseph was also addicted. He went to her and proposed that she should marry Joseph, and that he (the priest) would help them to live comfortably. Joseph, in order to live near his good master, consented also to marry the girl. Both knew very well what the other was. The banns were published during three Sabbaths, after which the old curate blessed the marriage of Joseph with the girl of his parishioner.

They lived together as husband and wife, in such harmony that nobody could suspect the horrible depravity which was concealed behind that union. Joseph continued, with his wife, to work often for his priest, till after some time that priest was removed, and another curate, called Tétreau, was sent in his place.

This new curate, knowing absolutely nothing of that mystery of iniquity, employed also Joseph and his wife, several times. One day, when Joseph was working at the door of the parsonage, in the presence of several people, a stranger arrived, and enquired of him if the Rev. Mr. Tétreau, the curate, was there.

Joseph answered "Yes, sir. But as you seem to be a stranger, would you allow me to ask you whence you come?"

"It is very easy, sir, to satisfy you. I come from Verchères," replied the stranger.

At the word "Verchères" Joseph turned so pale that the stranger could not but be struck with his sudden change of color.

Then, fixing his eyes on Joseph, he cried out. "Oh my God! what do I see here! Geneva! Geneva! I recognize you, and here you are in the disguise of a man!"

"Dear Uncle" (for it was her uncle), "for God's sake," she cried, "do not say a word more!"

But it was too late. The people, who were there, had heard the uncle and niece. Their long secret suspicions were well-founded—one of their former priests had kept a girl under the disguise of a man in his house! and, to blind his people more thoroughly, he had married that girl to another one, in order to have them both in his house when he pleased, without awakening any suspicion!

The news went almost as quick as lightning from one end to the other of the parish, and spread all over the northern country watered by the St. Lawrence River.

It is more easy to imagine than express the sentiments of surprise and horror which filled everyone. The justices of the peace took up the matter; Joseph was brought before the civil tribunal, which decided that a physician should be charged to make, not a post-mortem, but an ante-mortem inquest. The Honorable Laterière, who was called, and made the proper inquiry, declared that Joseph was a girl; and the bonds of marriage were legally dissolved.

During that time the honest Rev. Mr. Tétreau, struck with horror, had sent an express to the Right Reverend Bishop Coadjutor, of Quebec, informing him that the young man whom he had kept in his house several years, under the name of Joseph, was a girl.

Now, what were they to do with the girl, after all was discovered? Her presence in Canada would forever compromise the holy (?) Church of Rome. She knew too well how the priests, through the confessional, select their victims, and help themselves in their company, in keeping their solemn vows of celibacy! What would have become of the respect paid to the priest, if she had been taken by the hand and invited to speak bravely and boldly before the people of Canada?

The holy (?) Bishop and his vicars understood these things very well.

They immediately sent a trustworthy man with £500, to say to the girl that if she remained at Canada, she could be prosecuted and severely punished; that it was her interest to leave the country, and emigrate to the United States. They offered her the £500 if she would promise to go and never return.

She accepted the offer, crossed the lines, and has never gone back to Canada, where her sad history is well known by thousands and thousands.

In the providence of God I was invited to preach in that parish soon after, and I learned these facts accurately.

The Rev. Mr. Tétreau, under whose pastorate this great iniquity was detected, began from that time to have his eyes opened to the awful depravity of the priests of Rome through the confessional.

He wept and cried over his own degradation in the midst of that modern Sodom. Our merciful God looked down with compassion upon him, and sent him His saving grace. Not long after, he sent to the Bishop his renunciation of the errors and abominations of Romanism.

To-day he is working in the vineyard of the Lord with the Methodists in the city of Montreal, where he is ready to prove the correctness of what I say.*

Let those who have ears to hear, and eyes to see, understand, by this fact, that Pagan nations have not known any institution more depraving than Auricular Confession.

---

* This was written in 1874. Now, in 1880, I have to say that Rev. Mr. Tétreau died in 1877, in the peace of God, in Montreal. Twice before death he ordered out the priests of Rome, who had come to try to persuade him to make his peace with the Pope, calling them "Suppots de Satan"—"Devil's Messengers."

CHAPTER V

THE most skilful warrior has never had to display so much skill and so many ruses de guerre—he has never had to use more tremendous efforts to reduce and storm an impregnable citadel, than the confessor, who wants to reduce and storm the citadel of self-respect and honesty which God Himself has built around the soul and the heart of every daughter of Eve.

But, as it is through woman that the Pope wants to conquer the world, it is supremely important that he should enslave and degrade her by keeping her at his feet as his footstool, that she may become a passive instrument for the accomplishment of his vast and profound scheme.

In order perfectly to master women in the higher circles of society, every confessor is ordered by the Pope to learn the most complicated and perfect strategy. He has to study a great number of treatises on the art of persuading the fair sex to confess to him plainly, clearly, and in detail, every thought, every secret desire, word, and deed, just as they occurred.

And that art is considered so important and so difficult that all the theologians of Rome call it "the art of arts."

Dens, St. Liguori, Chevassu, the author of the "Mirror of the Clergy," Debreyne, and a multitude of authors too numerous to mention, have given the curious and scientific rules of that secret art.

They all agree in declaring that it is a most difficult and dangerous art; they all confess that the least error of judgment, the least imprudence or temerity, when storming the impregnable citadel, is certain death (spiritual, of course) to the confessor and the penitent.

The confessor is taught to make the first steps towards the citadel with the utmost caution, in order that his female penitent may not suspect at first, what he wants her to reveal; for that would generally induce her to shut for ever the door of the fortress against him. After the first steps of advance, he is advised to make several steps back, and to put himself in a kind of spiritual ambuscade, to see the effect of his first advance. If there is any prospect of success, then the word "March on!" is given, and a more advanced post of the citadel must be tried and stormed, if possible. In that way, little by little, the whole place is so well surrounded, so well crippled, denuded and dismantled, that any more resistance seems impossible on the part of the rebellious soul.

Then, the last charge is ordered, the final assault is made; and if God does not perform a real miracle to save that soul, the last walls crumble, the doors are beaten down; then the confessor makes a triumphant entry into the place; the very heart, soul, conscience, and intelligence are conquered.

When once master of the place, the priest visits all its most secret recesses and corners; he pries into its most sacred chamber. The conquered place is entirely and absolutely in his hands; he is the supreme master; for the surrender has been unconditional. The confessor has become the only infallible ruler in the conquered place—nay, he has become its only God—for it is in the name of God he has besieged, stormed and conquered it; it is in the name of God that, hereafter, he will speak and be obeyed.

No human words can adequately convey an idea of the irreparable ruin which follows the successful storming and unconditional surrender of that, once, noble fortress. The longer and stronger the resistance has been, the more terrible and complete is the destruction of its beauty and strength; the nobler the struggle has been, the more irretrievable are the ruin and loss. Just as the higher and stronger the dam is built to stem the current of the rapid and deep waters of the river, the more awful will be the disasters which follows its destruction; so it is with that noble soul. A mighty dam has been built by the very hand of God, called self-respect and womanly-modesty, to guard her against the pollutions of this sinful world; but the day that the priest of Rome succeeds, after long efforts, in destroying it, the soul is carried by an irresistible power into unfathomable abysses of iniquity. Then it is that the once respected lady will consent to hear, without a blush, things against which the most degraded woman would indignantly shut her ears. Then it is that she freely speaks with her confessor on matters, for reprinting which a printer in England has lately been sent to jail.

At first, in spite of herself, but soon with a real sensual pleasure, that fallen angel, when alone, will think on what she has heard, and what she has said in the confessional-box. Then, in spite of herself, the vilest thoughts will, at first irresistibly fill her mind; and soon the thoughts will engender temptations and sins. But those vile temptations and sins, which would have filled her with horror and regret before her entire surrender into the hands of the foe, beget very different sentiments, now that she is no more her own self-possessor and guide. The conviction of her sins is no more connected with the thought of a God, infinitely holy and just, whom she must serve and fear. The convictions of her sins is now immediately connected with the thought of a man with whom she will have to speak, and who will easily make everything right and pure in her soul by his absolution.

When the day for going to confession comes, instead of being sad, uneasy and bashful, as she used to be formerly, she feels pleased and delighted to have a new opportunity of conversing on those matters without impropriety and sin to herself; for she is now fully persuaded that there is no impropriety, no shame, no sin; nay, she believes, or tries to believe, that it is a good, honest, Christian, and godly thing to converse with her priest on those matters.

Her most happy hours are when she is at the feet of that spiritual physician, showing him all the newly-made wounds of her soul, and explaining all her constant temptations, her bad thoughts, her most intimate secret desires and sins.

Then it is that the most sacred mysteries of the married life are revealed; then it is that the mysterious and precious pearls which God has given as a crown of mercy to those whom He has made one body, one heart and soul, by the blessed ties of a Christian union, are lavishly thrown before swine.

Whole hours are passed by the fair penitent in thus speaking to her Father Confessor with the utmost freedom, on matters which would rank her amongst the most profligate and lost women, if it were only suspected by her friends and relatives. A single word of those intimate conversations would be followed by an act of divorce on the part of her husband, if it were known to him.

But the betrayed husband knows nothing of the dark mysteries of auricular confession; the duped father suspects nothing; a cloud from hell has obscured the intelligence of them both, and made them blind. On the contrary,—husbands and fathers, friends and relations, feel edified and pleased with the touching spectacle of the piety of Madam and Miss ——. In the village, as well as in the city, every one has a word to speak in their praise. Mrs. —— is so often seen humbly prostrated at the feet, or by the side, of her confessor; Miss —— remains so long in the confessional-box; they receive the holy communion so frequently; they both speak so eloquently and so often of the admirable piety, modesty, holiness, patience, charity, of their incomparable spiritual Father!

Every one congratulates them on their new and exemplary life, and they accept the compliment with the utmost humility, attributing their rapid progress in Christian virtues to the holiness of their confessor. He is such a spiritual man; who could not make rapid strides under such a holy guide?

The more constant the temptations, the more the secret sins overwhelm the soul, and the more airs of peace and holiness are put on. The more foul the secret emanations of the heart, the more the fair and refined penitent surrounds herself by an atmosphere of the sweetest perfumes of a sham piety. The more polluted the inside of the sepulchre is, the more shining and white the outside will be kept.

Then it is that, unless God performs a miracle to prevent it, the ruin of that soul is sealed. She has drunk in the poisonous cup filled by the "mother of harlots," she has found the wine of her prostitution sweet! She will henceforth delight in her spiritual and secret orgies.

Her holy (?) confessor has told her that there is no impropriety, no shame, no sin, in that cup. The Pope has sacrilegiously written the word "Life" on that cup of "Death." She has believed the Pope; the terrible mystery of iniquity is accomplished.

"The mystery of iniquity doth already work, whose coming is after the working of Satan with all power and signs and lying wonders, and with all deceivableness of unrighteousness in them that perish, because they received not the love of the truth that they might be saved. And for this cause God shall send them strong delusion, that they should believe a lie; that they all might be damned who believed not the truth, but had pleasure in unrighteousness." (2 Thess. ii. 7-12.)

Yes; the day that the rich, well-educated lady gives up her self-respect, and unconditionally surrenders the citadel of womanly modesty into the hands of a man, whatever be his name or titles, that he may freely put to her questions of the vilest character, which she must answer, she is lost and degraded, just as if she were the humblest and poorest servant-girl.

I purposely say "the rich and well-educated woman," for I know that there is a prevalent opinion that the social position of her class places her above the corrupting influences of the confessional, as if she were out of the reach of the common miseries of our poor fallen and sinful nature.

So long as the well-educated lady makes use of her accomplishments to defend the citadel of her womanly self-respect against the foe—so long as she sternly keeps the door of her heart shut against her deadly enemy—she is safe.

But let no one forget this: she is safe only so long as she does not surrender. When the enemy is once master of the place, I emphatically repeat, the ruinous consequences are as great, if not greater, and more irreparable than in the lowest classes of society. Throw a piece of precious gold into the mud, and tell me if it will not plunge deeper than the piece of rotten wood.

What woman could be nobler, purer, and stronger than Eve when she came from the hands of her Divine Creator? But how quickly she fell when she gave ear to the seducing voice of the tempter! How irreparable was her ruin when she complacently looked on the forbidden fruit, and believed the lying voice which told her there was "no sin" in eating of it!

I solemnly, in the presence of the great God, who ere long will judge me, give my testimony on this grave subject. After 25 years' experience in the confessional, I declare that the confessor himself encounters more terrible dangers when hearing the confessions of refined and highly educated ladies, than when listening to those of the humbler classes of his female penitents.

I solemnly testify that the well-educated lady, when she has once surrendered herself to the power of her confessor, becomes at least as vulnerable to the arrows of the enemy as the poorer and less educated. Nay, I must say that, once on the downhill road of perdition, the high-bred lady runs headlong into the pit with a more deplorable rapidity than her humbler sister.

All Canada is witness that a few years ago, it was among the highest ranks of society that the Grand Vicar Superior of the college of Montreal was choosing his victims, when the public cry of indignation and shame forced the Bishop to send him back to Europe, where he, soon after, died. Was it not also among the higher classes of society that a superior of the Seminary of Quebec was destroying souls, when he was detected, and forced, during a dark night, to fly and conceal himself behind the walls of the Trappist Monastery of Iowa?

Many would be the folio volumes which I should have to write, were I to publish all that my twenty-five years' experience in the confessional has taught me of the unspeakable secret corruption of the greatest part of the so-called respectable ladies, who have unconditionally surrendered themselves into the hands of their holy (?) confessors. But the following fact will suffice for those who have eyes to see, ears to hear, and an intelligence to understand:—

In one of the most beautiful and thriving towns along the St. Lawrence River, lived a rich merchant. He was young, and his marriage with a most lovely, rich, and accomplished young lady had made him one of the happiest men in the land.

A few years after his marriage, the Bishop appointed to that town a young priest, really remarkable for his eloquence, zeal, and amiable qualities; and the merchant and the priest soon became connected by links of the most sincere friendship.

The young, accomplished wife of the merchant soon became the model woman of the place under the direction of her new confessor.

Many and long were the hours she used to pass by the side of her spiritual father to be purified and enlightened by his godly advices. She soon was seen at the head of the few who had the privilege of receiving the holy communion once a week.

The husband, who was a good Roman Catholic himself, blessed God and the Virgin Mary, that he had the privilege of living with such an angel of piety.

Nobody had the least suspicion of what was going on under that holy and white mantle of the most exalted piety. Nobody, except God and His angels, could hear the questions put by the priest to his fair penitent, and the answers made during the long hours of their tête-a-tête in the confessional-box. Nobody but God could see the hellish fires which were devouring the hearts of the confessor and his victim! For nearly one year, both the young priest and his spiritual patient enjoyed, in those intimate and secret conversations, all the pleasure which lovers feel when they can speak freely to each other of their secret thoughts and love.

But this was not enough for them. They both wanted something more real; though the difficulties were great, and seemed insurmountable. The priest had his mother and sister with him, whose eyes were too sharp to allow him to invite the lady to his own house for any criminal object, and the young husband had no business, at a distance, which could keep him long enough out of his happy home to allow the Pope's confessor to accomplish his diabolical designs.

But when a poor fallen daughter of Eve has a mind to do a thing, she very soon finds the means, particularly if high education has added to her natural shrewdness.

And in this case, as in many others of a similar nature which have been revealed to me, she soon found out how to attain her object without compromising herself or her holy (?) confessor. A plan was soon found and cordially agreed to; and both patiently awaited their opportunity.

"Why have you not gone to mass to-day and received the holy communion, my dear?" said the husband. "I had ordered the servant-man to put the horse in the buggy for you, as usual."

"I am not very well, my beloved; I have passed a sleepless night from headache."

"I will send for the physician," replied the husband.

"Yes, my dear; do send for the physician—perhaps he will do me good."

One hour after the physician called, and he found his fair patient a little feverish, pronounced that there was nothing serious, and that she would soon be well. He gave her a little powder, to be taken three times a day, and left; but at 9 P.M., she complained of a great pain in the chest, and soon fainted and fell on the floor.

The doctor was again immediately sent for, but he was from home; it took nearly half an hour before he could come. When he arrived the alarming crisis was over—she was sitting in an arm-chair, with some neighboring women, who were applying cold water and vinegar to her forehead.

The physician was really at a loss what to say of the cause of such a sudden illness. At last, he said that it might be an attack of "ver solitaire" (tape-worm). He declared that it was not dangerous; that he knew how to cure her. He ordered some new powder to be taken, and left, after having promised to return the next day. Half an hour after, she began to complain of a most terrible pain in her chest, and fainted again; but before doing so, she said to her husband:—

"My dear, you see that the physician understands absolutely nothing of the nature of my disease. I have not the least confidence in him, for I feel that his powders make me worse. I do not want to see him any more. I suffer more than you suspect, my beloved; and if there is not soon a change, I may be dead to-morrow. The only physician I want is our holy confessor; please make haste to go and get him. I want to make a general confession, and to receive the holy viaticum (communion) and extreme unction before I grow worse."

Beside himself with anxiety, the distracted husband ordered the horse to be put in the buggy, and made his servant accompany him on horseback, to ring the bell, while his pastor carried "the good god" (Le Bon Dieu) to his dear sick wife.

He found the priest piously reading his breviarium (his book of daily prayers), and admired the charity and promptitude with which his good pastor, in that dark and chilly night, was ready to leave his warm and comfortable parsonage at the first appeal of the sick. In less than an hour, the husband had taken the priest with "the good god" from the church to the bedroom of his wife.

All along the way, the servant-man had rung a big hand-bell, to awaken the sleeping farmers, who, at the noise, had to jump, half naked, out of their beds, and worship, on their knees, with their faces prostrate in the dust, "the good god" which was being carried to the sick by the holy (?) priest.

On his arrival, the confessor, with every appearance of sincere piety, deposited "the good god" (Le Bon Dieu) on a table richly prepared for such a solemn occasion, and, approaching the bed, leaned his head towards his penitent, and inquired how she felt.

She answered him, "I am very sick, and I want to make a general confession before I die."

Speaking to her husband, she said, with a fainting voice, "Please, my dear, tell my friends to withdraw from the room, that I may not be distracted when making what may be my last confession."

The husband respectfully requested the friends to leave the room with him, and shut the door, that the holy confessor might be alone with his penitent during her general confession.

One of the most diabolical schemes, under the cover of auricular confession, had perfectly succeeded. The mother of harlots, the great enchantress of souls, whose seat is on the city of the "seven hills," had, there, her priest to bring shame, disgrace, and damnation, under the mask of Christianity.

The destroyer of souls, whose masterpiece is auricular confession, had, there, for the millionth time, a fresh opportunity of insulting the God of purity through one of the most criminal actions which the dark shades of night can conceal.

But let us draw the veil over the abominations of that hour of iniquity, and let us leave to hell its dark secrets.

After he had accomplished the ruin of his victim and most cruelly and sacrilegiously abused the confidence of his friend, the young priest opened the door of the room and said, with a sanctimonious air, "You may now enter to pray with me, while I give the last sacrament to our dear sick sister."

They came in: "the good god" (Le Bon Dieu) was given to the woman; and the husband, full of gratitude for the considerate attention of his priest, took him back to his parsonage, and thanked him most sincerely for having so kindly come to visit his wife in so chilly a night.

Ten years later I was called to preach a retreat (a kind of revival) in that same parish. That lady, then an absolute stranger to me, came to my confessional-box and confessed to me those details as I now give them. She seemed to be really penitent, and I gave her absolution and the entire pardon of her sins, as my Church told me to do. On the last day of the revival, the merchant invited me to a grand dinner. Then it was that I came to know who my penitent had been. I must not forget to mention that she had confessed to me that, of her four children, the last three belonged to her confessor! He had lost his mother, and, his sister having married, his parsonage had become more accessible to his fair penitents, many of whom had availed themselves of that opportunity to practice the lessons they had learned in the confessional. The priest had been removed to a higher position, where he, more than ever, enjoyed the confidence of his superiors, the respect of the people, and the love of his female penitents.

I never felt so embarrassed in my life as when at the table of that so cruelly victimized man. We had hardly begun to take our dinner when he asked me if I had known their late pastor, the amiable Rev. Mr. ——.

I answered, "Yes, I know him."

"Is he not a most accomplished priest?"

"Yes, sir, he is a most accomplished man," I answered.

"Why is it," rejoined the good merchant, "that the Bishop has taken him away from us? He was doing so well here; he had so deservedly earned the confidence of all by his piety and gentlemanly manners that we made every effort to keep him with us. I drew up a petition myself, which all the people signed to induce the Bishop to allow him to remain in our midst; but in vain. His lordship answered us that he wanted him for a more important place, on account of his rare ability, and we had to submit. His zeal and devotedness knew no bounds; in the darkest and most stormy nights he was always ready to come to the first call of the sick; I shall never forget how quickly and cheerfully he responded to my appeal when, a few years ago, I went, on one of our most chilly nights, to request him to visit my wife, who was very sick."

At this stage of the conversation, I must confess that I nearly laughed outright. The gratitude of that poor dupe of the confessional to the priest who had come to bring shame and destruction to his house, and the idea of that very man going himself to convey to his home the corruptor of his own wife, seemed to me so ludicrous that for a moment, I had to make a superhuman effort to control myself.

But I was soon brought to my better senses by the shame which I felt at the idea of the unspeakable degradation and secret infamy of the clergy of which I was a member. At that instant, hundreds of instances of similar, if not greater, depravity, which had been revealed to me through the confessional, came to my mind, and distressed and disgusted me so that my tongue was almost paralysed.

After dinner, the merchant asked his lady to call the children that I might see them, and I could not but admire their beauty. But I do not need to say that the pleasure of seeing these dear and lovely little ones was much marred by the secret, though sure, knowledge I had, that the three youngest were the fruits of the unspeakable depravity of auricular confession in the higher ranks of society.

CHAPTER VI

AURICULAR CONFESSION DESTROYS ALL THE SACRED
TIES OF MARRIAGE AND HUMAN SOCIETY

WOULD the banker allow his priest to open, when alone, the safe of his bank, manipulate and examine his papers, and pry into the most secret details of his banking business?

No! surely not.

How is it then, that the same banker allows that priest to open the heart of his wife, manipulate her soul, and pry into the sacred chambers of her most intimate and secret thoughts?

Are not the heart, the soul, the purity, and the self-respect of his wife as great and precious treasures as the safe of his bank! Are not the risks and dangers of temptations, imprudences, indiscretions, much greater and more irreparable in the second, than in the first case?

Would the jeweler or goldsmith allow his priest to come, when he pleases, and handle the rich articles of his stores, ransack the desk where the money is deposited, and play with it as he pleases?

No! surely not.

But are not the heart, the soul, and the purity of his dear wife and daughter a thousandfold more valuable than his precious stones, or silver and gold wares? Are not the dangers of temptation and indiscretions, on the part of the priest, more formidable and irresistible in the second, than in the first of these cases?

Would the livery man allow his priest to take his most valuable and unmanageable horses, when he wishes, and drive alone, without any other consideration and security than the discretion of his priest?

No! surely not.

That livery man knows that he would soon be ruined if he were to do so. Whatever may be his confidence in the discretion, honesty, and prudence of his priest, he will never push his confidence so far as to give him the unreserved control of the noble and fiery animals which are the glory of his stables and the support of his family.

How then, can the same man trust the entire, absolute management of his wife and dear daughters to the control of that one, to whom he would not entrust his horses?

Are not his wife and daughters as precious to him as those horses? Is there not greater danger of indiscretions, mismanagement, irreparable and fatal errors on the part of the priest, dealing alone with his wife and daughters, than when driving horses? No human act of folly, moral depravity, and want of common sense can equal the permission by a man to his wife to go and confess to the priest.

That day, he abdicates the loyal—I had almost said divine —dignity of husband; for it is from God that he holds it; his crown is forever lost, his sceptre broken!

What would you do to any one mean enough to peep or listen through the keyhole of your door in order to hear or see anything that was said or done within? Would you show so little self-respect as to tolerate such indiscretion? Would you not rather take a whip or a cane, and drive away the villain? Would you not even expose your life to free yourself from his impudent curiosity?

But what is the confessional if not the key-hole of your house and of your very chamber, through which the priest can hear and see your most secret words and actions; nay, more, know your most intimate thoughts and aspirations.

Are you worthy of the name of men when you submit yourselves to such sly and insulting inquisition? Do you deserve the name of men, who consent to put up with such ignoble affront and humiliation?

"The husband is the head of the wife even as Christ is the Head of the Church." "Therefore, as the Church is subject unto Christ, so let the wives be to their own husbands in everything" —(Eph. v). If these solemn words are the true oracles of divine wisdom, is not the husband divinely appointed the only advisor, counsellor, help of his wife, just as Christ is the only adviser, counsellor, and help of His Church?

If the Apostle was not an impostor when he said that the wife is to her husband what the body is to the head, and that the husband is to his wife what the head is to the body—is not the husband appointed by God to be the light, the guide, of his wife? Is it not his duty, as well as his privelege and glory, to console her in her afflictions, strengthen her in her hours of weakness, keep her up when she is in danger of fainting, and encourage her when she is on the rough and uphill ways of life?

If Christ has not come to deceive the world through his Apostle, must not the wife go to her husband for advice? Ought she not to expect from him, and him alone, after God, the light she wants and the consolation she is in need of? Is it not to her husband, and to him alone, after God, she ought to look to in her days of trial for help? Is it not under his leadership alone she must fight the battle of life and conquer?

Is not this mutual and daily sharing of the anxieties of life, this constant shouldering on the battle-field, and this reciprocal and mutual protection and help renewed at every hour of the day, which form, under the eyes and by the mercy of God, the holiest and the purest charms of the married life? Is it not that unreserved confidence in each other which binds together those golden links of Christian love that make them happy in the very midst of the trials of life? Is it not through this mutual confidence alone that they are one as God wants them to be one? Is it not in this unity of thoughts, fears and hopes, joys and love, which come from God, that they can cheerfully cross the thorny valley, and safely reach the Promised land?

The Gospel says that the husband is to his wife what Christ is to His Church! Is it not, then, a most sacrilegious iniquity for a wife to look to another rather than to her own husband for such advice, wisdom, strength, and life, as he is entitled, qualified, and ready to afford? As no other man has the right to her love, so no other man has any right to her absolute confidence. As she becomes an adulteress the day that she gives her body to another man, is she any the less an adulteress the day that she gives her confidence and trusts her soul to a stranger? The adultery of the heart and soul is not less criminal than the adultery of the body; and every time the wife goes to the feet of the priest to confess, does she not become guilty of that iniquity?

In the Church of Rome, through the confessional, the priest is much more the husband of the wife than the man to whom she was wedded at the foot of the altar. The priest has the best part of the wife. He has the marrow, when the husband has the bones. He has the juice of the orange, the husband has the rind. He has the soul and the heart, the husband has the skeleton. He has the honey, the husband has the wax cell. He has the succulent oyster, the husband has the dry shell. As much as the soul is higher than the body, so much are the power and privileges of the priest higher than the power and privileges of the husband in the mind of the penitent wife. As the husband is the lord of the body which he feeds, so the priest is the lord of the soul and the heart, which he also feeds. The wife, then, has two lords and masters, whom she must love, respect and obey. Will she not give the best part of her love, respect, and submission to the one who, in her mind, is as much above the other as the heavens are above the earth? But as she cannot serve two masters together, will not the master who prepares and fits her for an eternal life of glory, certainly be the object of her constant, real, and most ardent love, gratitude, and respect, when the worldly and sinful man to whom she is married, will have only the appearance and the crumbs of those sentiments? Will she not naturally, instinctively serve, love, respect, and obey, as lord and master, the godly man, whose yoke is so light, so holy, so divine, rather than the carnal man, whose human imperfections are to her a source of daily trial and suffering?

In the Church of Rome, the thoughts and desires, the secret joys and fears of the soul, the very life of the wife, are sealed things to the husband. He has no right to look into the sanctuary of her heart; he has no remedy to apply to the soul; he has no mission from God to advise her in the dark hours of her anxieties; has no balm to apply to the bleeding wounds, so often received in the daily battles of life; he must remain a perfect stranger in his own house.

The wife, expecting nothing from her husband, has no revelation to make to him, no favor to ask, no debt of gratitude to pay. Nay, she shuts all the avenues of her soul, all the doors and windows of her heart, against her husband. The priest, and the priest alone, has a right to her entire confidence; to him, and him alone, she will go and reveal all her secrets, show all her wounds; to him, and him alone, she will turn her mind, her heart and soul, in the hour of trouble and anxiety; from him, and him, alone, she will ask and expect the light and consolation she wants. Every day, more and more, her husband will become a stranger to her, if he does not become a real nuisance, and an obstacle to her happiness and peace.

Yes, through the confessional, an unfathomable abyss has been dug by the Church of Rome, between the heart of the wife and the heart of the husband. Their bodies may be very near each other, but their souls, their real affections and their confidence are at greater distance than the north is from the south pole of the earth. The confessor is the master, the ruler, the king of the soul; the husband, as the graveyard-keeper, must be satisfied with the carcass!

The husband has the permission to look on the outside of the palace; he is allowed to rest his head on the cold marble of the outdoor steps; but the confessor triumphantly walks into the mysterious starry rooms, examines at leisure their numberless and unspeakable wonders; and alone, he is allowed to rest his head on the soft pillows of the unbounded confidence, respect, and love of the wife.

In the Church of Rome, if the husband ask a favor from his wife, nine times in ten she will inquire from her father confessor whether or not she can grant him his request; and the poor husband will have to wait patiently for the permission of the master, or the rebuke of the lord, according to the answer of the oracle which had to be consulted! If he gets impatient under the yoke, and murmurs, the wife will, soon, go to the feet of her confessor, to tell him how she has the misfortune to be united to a most unreasonable man, and how she has to suffer from him! She reveals to her "dear father" how she is unhappy under such a yoke, and how her life would be an insupportable burden, had she not the privilege and happiness of coming often to his feet, to lay down her sorrows, hear his sympathetic words, and get his so affectionate and paternal advice! She tells him, with tears of gratitude, that it is only when by his side, and at his feet, she finds rest to her weary soul, balm to her bleeding heart, and peace to her troubled conscience.

When she comes from the confessional, her ears are long filled as with a heavenly music: the honied words of her confessor ring for many days in her heart: she feels it lonesome to be separated from him: his image is constantly before her mind, and the souvenir of his amiabilities is one of her most pleasant thoughts. There is nothing which she likes so much as to speak of his good qualities, his patience, his piety, his charity; she longs for the day when she will again go to confess and pass a few hours by the side of that angelic man, in opening to him all the secrets of her heart, and in revealing all her ennuis. She tells him how she regrets that she cannot come oftener to see him, and receive the benefits of his charitable counsels; she does not even conceal from him how often, in her dreams, she feels so happy to be with him! More and more every day the gap between her and her husband widens. More and more each day she regrets that she has not the happiness to be the wife of such a holy man as her confessor! Oh! if it were possible——! But then, she blushes or smiles and sings a song.

Then again, I ask, Who is the true lord, ruler and master in that house? For whom does that heart beat and live?

Thus it is that that stupendous imposture, the dogma of auricular confession, does completely destroy all the links, the joys, the responsibilities, and divine privileges of the married life, and transforms it into a life of perpetual, though disguised, adultery. It becomes utterly impossible, in the Church of Rome, that the husband should be one with his wife, and that the wife should be one with her husband: a "monstrous being" has been put between them both, called the confessor. Born in the darkest ages of the world, that being has received from hell his mission to destroy and contaminate the purest joys of the married life, to enslave the wife, to outrage the husband, and to damn the world!

The more auricular confession is practiced, the more the laws of public and private morality are trampled under foot. The husband wants his wife to be his—he does not, and could not, consent to share his authority over her with anybody: he wants to be the only man who will have her confidence and her heart, as well as her respect and love. And so, the very moment that he anticipates the dark shadow of the confessor coming between him and the woman of his choice, he prefers to shrink from entering into the sacred bond; the holy joys of home and family lose their divine attractions; he prefers the cold life of an ignominious celibacy to the humiliation and opprobrium of the questionable privileges of an uncertain paternity.

France, Spain, and many other Roman Catholic countries, thus witness the multitude of those bachelors increasing every year. The number of families and births, in consequence, is fast decreasing in their midst; and, if God does not perform a miracle to stop these nations in their downward course, it is easy to calculate the day when they will owe their existence to the tolerance and pity of the mighty Protestant nations which surround them.

Why is it that the Irish Roman Catholic people are so irreparably degraded and clothed in rags? Why is it that that people, whom God has endowed with so many noble qualities, seem to be so deprived of intelligence and self-respect that they glory in their own shame? Why is it that their land has been for centuries the land of bloody riots and cowardly murders? The principal cause is the enslaving of the Irish women, by means of the confessional. Every one knows that the spiritual slavery and degradation of the Irish woman has no bounds. After she has been enslaved and degraded, she, in turn, has enslaved and degraded her husband and her sons. Ireland will be an object of pity; she will be poor, miserable, riotous, bloodthirsty, degraded, so long as she rejects Christ, to be ruled by the father confessor, planted in every parish by the Pope.

Who has not been amazed and saddened by the downfall of France? How is it that her once so mighty armies have melted away, that her brave sons have so easily been conquered and disarmed? How is it that France, fallen powerless at the feet of her enemies, has frightened the world by the spectacle of the incredible, bloody, and savage follies of the Commune? Do not look for the causes of the downfall, humiliation, and untold miseries of France anywhere else than in the confessional. For centuries has not that great country obstinately rejected Christ? Has she not slaughtered or sent into exile her noblest children, who wanted to follow the Gospel? Has she not given her fair daughters into the hands of the confessors, who have defiled and degraded them? How could woman, in France, teach her husband and sons to love liberty, and die for it, when she was herself a miserable, an abject slave? How could she form her husband and sons to the manly virtues of heroes, when her own mind was defiled and her heart corrupted by the priest?

The French woman had unconditionally surrendered the noble and fair citadel of her heart, intelligence, and womanly self-respect into the hands of her confessor long before her sons surrendered their swords to the Germans at Sedan and Paris. The first unconditional surrender had brought the second.

The complete moral destruction of woman by the confessor in France has been a long work. It has required centuries to bow down, break, and enslave the noble daughters of France. Yes; but those who know France, know that that destruction is now as complete as it is deplorable. The downfall of woman in France, and her supreme degradation through the confessional, is now un fait accompli, which nobody can deny; the highest intellects have seen and confessed it. One of the most profound thinkers of that unfortunate country, Michelet, has depicted that supreme and irretrievable degradation in a most eloquent book, "The Priest, The Woman, The Family!" and not a voice has been raised to deny or refute what he had said. Those who have any knowledge of history and philosophy know very well that the moral degradation of the woman is soon followed everywhere by the moral degradation of the nation, and the moral degradation of the nation is very soon followed by ruin and overthrow.

The French nation had been formed by God to be a race of giants. They were chivalrous and brave; they had bright intelligences, stout hearts, strong arms and a mighy sword. But as the hardest granite rock yields and breaks under the drop of water which incessantly falls upon it, so that great nation had to break and to fall into pieces under, not the drop, but the rivers of impure waters which, for centuries, have incessantly flowed in upon it from the pestilential fountain of the confessional. "Righteousness exalteth a nation, but sin is a reproach to any people." (Proverbs xiv.)

In the sudden changes and revolutions of these latter days, France is also sharing; and the Church of Rome has received a blow there, which, though perhaps only temporary in its character, will help to awaken the people to the corruption and fraud of the priesthood.

Why is it that Spain is so miserable, so weak, so poor, so foolishly and cruelly, tearing her own bosom, and reddening her fair valley with the blood of her own children? The principal, if not the only, cause of the downfall of that great nation is the confessional. There, also, the confessor has defiled, degraded, enslaved women, and women in turn have defiled and degraded their husbands and sons. Women have sown broadcast over their country the seeds of that slavery, of that want of Christian honesty, justice, and self-respect with which they had themselves been first imbued in the confessional.

But when you see, without a single exception, the nations whose women drink the impure and poisonous waters, which flow from the confessional, sinking down so rapidly, do you not wonder how fast the neighboring nations, who have destroyed those dens of impurity, prostitution, and abject slavery, are rising up? What a marvellous contrast is before our eyes? On one side, the nations who allow the women to be degraded and enslaved at the feet of her confessor — France, Spain, Romish Ireland, Mexico, &c., &c.—are, there, fallen into the dust, bleeding, struggling, powerless, like the sparrow whose entrails are devoured by the vulture.

On the other side, see how the nations whose women go to wash their robes in the blood of the Lamb, are soaring up, as on eagle wings, in the highest regions of progress, peace, and liberty!

If legislators could once understand the respect and protection they owe to women, they would soon, by stringent laws, prohibit auricular confession as contrary to good morals and the welfare of society; for, though the advocates of auricular confession have succeeded, to a certain extent, in blinding the public, and in concealing the abominations of the system under a lying mantle of holiness and religion, it is nothing else than a school of impurity.

I say more than that. After twenty-five years of hearing the confessions of the common people and of the highest classes of society, of the laymen and the priests, of the grand vicars and bishops and the nuns; I conscientiously say before the world, that the immorality of the confessional is of a more dangerous and degrading nature than that which we attribute to the social evil of our great cities. The injury caused to the intelligence and to the soul in the confessional, as a general rule, is of a more dangerous nature and more irremediable, because it is neither suspected nor understood by its victims.

The unfortunate woman who lives an immoral life knows her profound misery; she often blushes and weeps over her degradation; she hears, from every side, voices which call her out of those ways of perdition. Almost at every hour of day and night, the cry of her conscience warns her against the desolation and suffering of an eternity passed far away from the regions of holiness, light, and life. All those things are often so many means of grace, in the hands of our merciful God, to awaken the mind, and to save the guilty soul. But in the confessional the poison is administered under the name of a pure and refreshing water; the deadly blow is inflicted by a sword so well oiled that the wound is not felt; the vilest and most impure notions and thoughts, in the form of questions and answers, are presented and accepted as the bread of life! All the notions of modesty, purity, and womanly self-respect and delicacy, are set aside and forgotten to propitiate the god of Rome. In the confessional the woman is told, and she believes, that there is no sin for her in hearing things which would make the vilest blush—no sin to say things which would make the most desperate villain on the streets of London to stagger—no sin to converse with her confessor on matters so filthy that, if attempted in civil life, would forever exclude the perpetrator from the society of the virtuous.

Yes, the soul and the intelligence defiled and destroyed in the confessional are often hopelessly defiled and destroyed. They are sinking into a complete, an irretrievable perdition; for, not knowing the guilt, they will not cry for mercy—not suspecting the fatal disease that is being fostered, they will not call for the true Physician. It was, evidently, when thinking of the unspeakable ruin of the souls of men through the wickedness culminating in the Pope's confessors, that the Son of God said:—"If the blind lead the blind, both shall fall into the ditch." To every woman, with very few exceptions, coming out from the feet of her confessor, the children of light may say:—"I know thy works, that thou hast a name that thou livest, but thou art dead—(Revelations iii.).

Nobody has yet been, nor ever will be able to answer the few following lines, which I addressed some years ago to the Rev. Mr. Bruyère, Roman Catholic Vicar-General of London, Canada:—

"With a blush on my face, and regret in my heart, I confess, before God and man, that I have been like you, and with you, through the confessional, plunged for twenty-five years in that bottomless sea of iniquity, in which the blind priests of Rome have to swim day and night.

"I had to learn by heart, like you, the infamous questions which the Church of Rome forces every priest to learn. I had to put those impure, immoral questions to old and young females, who were confessing their sins to me. These questions—you know it—are of such a nature that no prostitute would dare to put them to another. Those questions, and the answers they elicit, are so debasing that no man in London—you know it—

except a priest of Rome, is sufficiently lost to every sense of shame, as to put them to any woman.

"Yes, I was bound, in conscience, as you are bound to-day, to put into the ears, the mind, the imagination, the memory, the heart and soul of females, questions of such a nature, the direct and immediate tendency of which—you know it well—is to fill the minds and the hearts of both priests and female penitents with thoughts, phantoms, and temptations of such a degrading nature, that I do not know any words adequate to express them. Pagan antiquity has never seen any institution more polluting than the confessional. I know nothing more corrupting than the law which forces a female to tell her thoughts, desires, and most secret feelings and actions to an unmarried priest. The confessional is a school of perdition. You may deny that before the Protestants; but you cannot deny it before me. My dear Mr. Bruyère, if you call me a degraded man, because I have lived twenty-five years in the atmosphere of the confessional, you are right. I was a degraded man, just as yourself and all the priests are to-day, in spite of your denegations. If you call me a degraded man because my soul, my mind, and my heart were, as your own are to-day, plunged into the deep waters of iniquity which flow from the confessional, I confess, 'Guilty!' I was degraded and polluted by the confessional just as you and all the priests of Rome are.

"It has required the whole blood of the great Victim, who died on Calvary for sinners, to purify me; and I pray that, through the same blood, you may be purified also."

If the legislators knew the respect and protection they owe to women—I repeat it—they would, by the most stringent laws, prohibit auricular confession as a crime against society.

Not long ago, a printer in England was sent to jail and severely punished for having published in English the questions put by the priest to the women in the confessional; and the sentence was equitable, for all who will read those questions will conclude that no girl or woman who brings her mind into contact with the contents of that book can escape from moral death. But what are the priests of Rome doing in the confessional? Do they not pass the greatest part of their time in questioning females, old and young, and hearing their answers, on those very matters? If it were a crime, punishable by law, to present those questions in a book, is it not a crime far more punishable by law to present those very things to married and unmarried women through the auricular confession?

I ask it from every man of common sense. What is the difference between a woman or a girl learning those things in a book, or learning them from the lips of a man? Will not those impure, demoralizing suggestions sink more deeply into their minds, and impress themselves more forcibly in their memory, when told to them by a man of authority speaking in the name of Almighty God, than when read in a book which has no authority?

I say to the legislators of Europe and America, "Read for yourselves those horrible, unmentionable things;" and remember that the Pope has more than 100,000 priests whose principal work is to put those very things into the intelligence and memory of the women whom they entrap into their snares. Let us suppose that each priest hears the confessions of only five female penitents every day (though we know that the daily average is ten): it gives the awful number of 500,000 women whom the priests of Rome have the legal right to pollute and destroy each day of the year!

Legislators of the so-called Christian and civilized nations! I ask it again from you, Where is your consistency, your justice, your love of public morality, when you punish so severely the man who has printed the questions put to the woman in the confessional, while you honor and let free, and often pay the men whose public and private life is spent in spreading the very same moral poison in a much more efficacious, scandalous, and shameful way, under the mask of religion?

The confessional is in the hands of the devil, what West Point is to the United States, and Woolwich is to great Britain, a training of the army to fight and conquer the enemy. It is in the confessional that 500,000 women every day, and 182,000,000 every year, are trained by the Pope in the art of fighting against God, by destroying themselves and the whole world, through every imaginable kind of impurity and filthiness.

Once more, I request the legislators, the husbands, and the fathers in Europe, as well as in America and Australia, to read in Dens, Liguori, Debreyne, in every theological book of Rome, what their wives and their daughters have to learn in the confessional.

In order to screen themselves, the priests of Rome have recourse to the following miserable subterfuge:—"Is not the physician forced," they say, "to perform certain delicate operations on women? Do you complain of this? No! you let the physicians alone; you do not abuse them in their arduous and conscientious duties. Why, then, should you insult the physician of the soul, the confessor, in the accomplishment of his holy, though delicate duties?"

I answer, first, The art and science of the physician are approved and praised in many parts of the Scriptures. But the art and science of the confessor are nowhere to be found in the holy records. Auricular confession is nothing else than a most stupendous imposture. The filthy and impure questions of the confessor, with the polluting answers they elicit, were put among the most diabolical and forbidden actions by God Himself, the day that the Spirit of Truth, Holiness, and Life wrote the imperishable words—"Let no corrupt communication proceed out of your mouth." (Eph. iv. 29.)

Secondly, The physician is not bound by a solemn oath to remain ignorant of the things which it will be his duty to examine and cure. But the priest of Rome is bound, by the most ridiculous and impious oath of celibacy, to remain ignorant of the very things which are the daily objects of his inquiries, observation, and thoughts! The priest of Rome has sworn never to taste of the fruits with which he feeds his imagination, his memory, his heart, and his soul day and night! The physician is honest in the performance of his duties; but the priest of Rome becomes, in fact, a perjured man, every time he enters the confessional-box.

Thirdly, if a lady has a little sore on her small finger, and is obliged to go to the physician for a remedy, she has only to show her little finger, allow the plaster or ointment to be applied, and all is finished. The physician never—no never—says to that lady, "It is my duty to suspect that you have many other parts of your body which are sick; I am bound in conscience, under pain of death, to examine you from head to foot, in order to save your precious life from those secret diseases, which may kill you if they are not cured just now. Several of those diseases are of such a nature that you never dared perhaps to examine them with the attention they deserve, and you are hardly conscious of them. I know, madam, that this is a very painful and delicate thing for both you and me, that I should be forced to make that thorough examination of your person; however, there is no help; I am in duty bound to do it. But you have nothing to fear. I am a holy man, who have made a vow of celibacy. We are alone; neither your husband nor your father will ever know the secret infirmities I may find in you: they will never even suspect the perfect investigation I will make, and they will, forever, be ignorant of the remedy I will apply."

Has any physician ever been authorized to speak or act in this way with any of his female patients? No,—never! never!

But this is just the way the spiritual physician, by whom the devil enslaves and corrupts women, acts. When the fair, honest, and timid spiritual patient has come to her confessor, to show him the little sore she has on the small finger of her soul, the confessor is bound in conscience to suspect that she has other sores—secret, shameful sores! Yes, he is bound, nine times out of ten; and he is always allowed to suppose that she does not dare to reveal them! Then he is advised by the Church to induce her to let him search every corner of the heart, and of the soul, and to inquire about all kinds of contaminations, impurities, secret, shameful, and unspeakable matters! The young priest is drilled in the diabolical art of going into the most sacred recesses of the soul and the heart, almost in spite of his penitents. I could bring hundreds of theologians as witnesses to the truth of what I here say: but it is enough just now to cite three:—

"Lest the confessor should indolently hesitate in tracing out the circumstances of any sin, let him have the following versicle of circumstances in readiness:

"Quis, quid, ubi, quibus auxiliis, cur, quomodo quando. Who, which, where, with whom, why, how, when." (Dens, vol. 6, p. 123. Liguori, vol. 2, p. 464.)

The celebrated book of the Priests, "The Mirror of the Clergy," page 357, says:

"Oportet ut Confessor solet cognoscere quid quid debet judicare. Deligens igitur inquisitor et subtillis investigator sapienter, quasi astute, interrogat a peccatore quod ignorat, vel verecundia volit occultare."

"It is necessary that the confessor should know everything on which he has to exercise his judgment. Let him then, with wisdom and subtility, interrogate the sinners on the sins which they may ignore, or conceal through shame!"

The poor unprotected girl is, thus, thrown into the power of the priest, soul and body, to be examined on all the sins she may ignore, or which, through shame, she may conceal! On what a boundless sea of depravity the poor fragile bark is launched by the priest! On what bottomless abysses of impurities she will have to pass and travel, in company with the priest alone, before he will have interrogated her on all the sins she may ignore, or which she may have concealed through shame!! Who can tell the sentiments of surprise, shame, and distress, of a timid, honest, young girl, when, for the first time, she is initiated, through those questions, to infamies which are ignored even in houses of prostitution!!!

But such is the practice, the sacred duty of the spiritual physician. "Let him (the priest confessor), with wisdom and subtlety, interrogate the sinners on the sins they may ignore or conceal through shame."

And there are more than 100,000 men, not only allowed, but petted, and often paid by so-called Protestant, Christian, and civilised governments to do that under the name of the God of the Gospel!

Fourthly, I answer to the sophism of the priest: When the physician has any delicate and dangerous operation to perform on a female patient, he is never alone; the husband, or the father, the mother, the sister, or some friends of the patient are there, whose ·scrutinising eyes and attentive ears make it impossible for the physician to say or do any improper thing.

But when the poor, deluded spiritual patient comes to be treated by her so-called spiritual physician, and shows him her disease, is she not alone—shamefully alone—with him? Where are the protecting ears of the husband, the father, the mother, the sisters, or the friends? Where is the barrier interposed between this sinful, weak, tempted, and often depraved man and his victim!

Would the priest so freely ask this and that from a married woman, if he knew that her husband could hear him? No, surely not! for he is well aware that the enraged husband would blow out the brains of the villain who, under the sacrilegious pretext of purifying the soul of his wife, is filling her breast with every kind of pollution and infamy.

Fifthly, When the physician performs a delicate operation on one of his female patients, the operation is usually accompanied with pain, cries, and often with bloodshed. The sympathetic and honest physician suffers almost as much pain as his patient; those cries, acute pains, tortures, and bleeding wounds make it morally impossible that the physician should be tempted to any improper thing.

But the sight of the spiritual wounds of that fair penitent! Is the poor depraved human heart really sorry to see and examine them? Oh, no! it is just the contrary.

The dear Saviour weeps over those wounds; the angels are distressed at the sight. Yes! But the deceitful and corrupt heart of man! is it not rather apt to be pleased at the sight of wounds which are so much like the ones he has himself so often been pleased to receive from the hand of the enemy?

Was the heart of David pained and horror-struck at the sight of the fair Bathsheba, when, imprudently, and too freely, exposed in her bath? Was not that holy prophet smitten, and brought down to the dust, by that guilty look? Was not the mighty giant, Samson, undone by the charms of Delilah? Was not the wise Solomon ensnared and befooled in the midst of the women by whom he was surrounded?

Who will believe that the bachelors of the Pope are made of stronger metal than the Davids, the Samsons and the Solomons? Where is the man who has so completely lost his common sense as to believe that the priests of Rome are stronger than Samson, holier than David, wiser than Solomon? Who will believe that confessors will stand up on their feet amidst the storms which prostrate in the dust those giants of the armies of the Lord? To suppose that, in the generality of cases, the confessor can resist the temptations by which he is daily surrounded in the confessional, that he will constantly refuse the golden opportunities, which offer themselves to him, to satisfy the almost irresistible propensities of his fallen human nature, is neither wisdom nor charity; it is simply folly.

I do not say that all the confessors and their female penitents fall into the same degree of abject degradation; thanks be to God, I have known several, who nobly fought their battles, and conquered on that field of so many shameful defeats. But these are the exceptions. It is just as when the fire has ravaged one of our grand forests of America—how sad it is to see the numberless noble trees fallen under the devouring element! But, here and there, the traveler is not a little amazed and pleased, to find some which have proudly stood the fiery trial, without being consumed.

Was not the world at large struck with terror, when they heard of the fire which, a few years ago, reduced the great city of Chicago to ashes! But those who have visited that doomed city, and seen the desolating ruins of her 16,000 houses, had to stand in silent admiration before a few, which, in the very midst of an ocean of fire, had escaped untouched by the destructive element.

It is a fact, that owing to a most marvelous protection of God, some privileged souls, here and there, do escape the fatal destruction which overtakes so many others in the confessional.

The confessional is like the spider's web. How many too unsuspecting flies find death, when seeking rest on the beautiful framework of their deceitful enemy! How few escape! and this only after a most desperate struggle. See how the perfidious spider looks harmless in his retired, dark corner; how motionless he is; how patiently he waits for his opportunity! But look how quickly he surrounds his victim with his silky, delicate, and imperceptible links! how mercilessly he sucks its blood and destroys its life!

What remains of the imprudent fly, after she has been entrapped into the nets of her foe? Nothing but a skeleton. So it is with your fair wife, your precious daughter; nine times out of ten, nothing but a moral skeleton returns to you, after the Pope's black spider has been allowed to suck the very blood of her heart and soul. Let those who would be tempted to think that I exaggerate, read the following extracts from the memoirs of the Venerable Scipio de Ricci, Roman Catholic Bishop of Pistoia and Prato, in Italy. They were published by the Roman Catholic Italian Government, to show to the world that some measures had to be taken, by the civil and ecclesiastical authorities, to prevent the nation from being entirely swept away by the deluge of corruption flowing from the confessional, even among the most perfect of Rome's followers, the monks and the nuns. The priests have never dared to deny a single iota of these terrible revelations. On page 115 we read the following letter from sister Flavia Peraccini, Prioress of St. Catharine, to Dr. Thomas Camparina, Rector of the Episcopal Seminary of Pistoia:—

"In compliance with the request which you made me this day, I hasten to say something, but I know not how.

"Of those who have gone out of the world, I shall say nothing. Of those who are still alive and have very little decency of conduct, there are many, among whom there is an ex-provincial named Father Dr. Ballendi, Calvi, Zoratti, Bigliaci, Guidi, Miglieti, Verde, Rianchi, Ducci, Seraphini, Bolla, Nera di Luca, Quaretti, &c. But wherefore any more? With the exception of three or four, all those whom I have ever known, alive or dead, are of the same character; they have all the same maxims and the same conduct.

"They are on more intimate terms with the nuns than if they were married to them! I repeat it, it would require a great deal of time to tell half of what I know. It is the custom now, when they come to visit and hear the confession of a sick sister, to sup with the nuns, sing, dance, play, and sleep in the convent. It is a maxim of theirs that God has forbidden hatred, but not love; and that man is made for woman and woman for man.

"I say that they can deceive the innocent and the most prudent and circumspect, and that it would be a miracle to converse with them and not fall!"

Page 117.—"The priests are the husbands of the nuns, and the lay brothers of the lay sisters. In the chamber of one of the nuns I have mentioned, a man was one day found; he fled away but, soon after, they gave him to us as our confessor extraordinary.

"How many bishops are there in the Papal States who have come to the knowledge of those disorders, have held examinations and visitations, and yet never could remedy it, because the monks, our confessors, tell us that those are excommunicated who reveal what passes in the Order!

"Poor creatures! they think they are leaving the world to escape dangers, and they only meet with greater ones. Our fathers and mothers have given us a good education, and here we have to unlearn and forget what they have taught us."

Page 188.—"Do not suppose that this is the case in our convent alone. It is just the same at St. Lucia, Prato, Pisa, Perugia, &c. I have known things that would astonish you. Everywhere it is the same. Yes, everywhere the same disorders, the same abuses prevail. I say, and I repeat it, let the superiors suspect as they may, they do not know the smallest part of the enormous wickedness that goes on between the monks and the nuns whom they confess. Every monk who passed by on his way to the chapter, entreated a sick sister to confess to him, and——!"

Page 119.—"With respect to Father Buzachini, I say that he acted just as the others, sitting up late in the nunnery, diverting himself, and letting the usual disorders go on. There were several nuns who had love affairs on his account. His own principal mistress was Odaldi, of St. Lucia, who used to send him continual treats. He was also in love with the daughter of our factor, of whom they were very jealous here. He ruined also poor Cancellieri, who was sextoness. The monks are all alike with their penitents.

"Some years ago, the nuns of St. Vincent, in consequence of the extraordinary passion they had for their father confessors Lupi and Borghini, were divided into two parties, one calling themselves Le Lupe, the other Le Borghiani.

"He who made the greatest noise was Donati. I believe he is now at Rome. Father Brandi, too, was also in great vogue. I think he is now Prior of St. Gemignani. At St. Vincent, which passes for a very holy retreat, they have also their lovers——."

My pen refuses to reproduce several things which the nuns of Italy have published against their father confessors. But this is enough to show to the most incredulous that the confession is nothing else but a school of perdition, even among those who make a profession to live in the highest regions of Roman Catholic holiness—the monks and the nuns.

Now, from Italy let us go to America and see again the working of auricular confession, not between the holy (?) nuns and monks of Rome, but among the humblest classes of country women and priests. Great is the number of parishes where women have been destroyed by their confessors, but I will speak only of one.

When curate of Beauport, I was called by the Rev. Mr. Proulx, curate of St. Antoine, to preach a retreat (a revival) with the Rev. Mr. Aubry, to his parishioners, and eight or ten other priests were also invited to come and help us to hear the confessions.

The very first day, after preaching and passing five or six hours in the confessional, the hospitable curate gave us a supper before going to bed. But it was evident that a kind of uneasiness pervaded the whole company of the father confessors. For my own part I could hardly raise my eyes to look at my neighbor; and, when I wanted to speak a word, it seemed that my tongue was not free as usual; even my throat was as if it were choked: the articulation of the sounds was imperfect. It was evidently the same with the rest of the priests. Instead, then, of the noisy and cheerful conversations of the other meals, there were only a few insignificant words exchanged with a half-suppressed tone.

The Rev. Mr. Proulx (the curate) at first looked as if he also were partaking of that singular, though general, despondent feeling. During the first part of the lunch he hardly said a word; but, at last, raising his head, and turning his honest face towards us, in his usual gentlemanly, and cheerful manner, he said:

"Dear friends, I see that you are all under the influence of the most painful feelings. There is a burden on you that you can neither shake off nor bear as you wish. I know the cause of your trouble, and I hope you will not find fault with me, if I help you to recover from that disagreeable mental condition. You have heard, in the confessional, the history of many great sins; but I know that this is not what troubles you. You are all old enough in the confessional to know the miseries of poor human nature. Without any more preliminaries, I will come to the subject. It is no more a secret in this place, that one of the priests who has preceded me, has been very unfortunate, weak, and guilty with the greatest part of the married women whom he has confessed. Not more than one in ten has escaped him. I would not mention this fact had I got it only from the confessional, but I know it well from other sources, and I can speak of it freely, without breaking the secret seal of the confessional. Now, what troubles you is that, probably, when a great number of those women have confessed to you what they had done with their confessor, you have not asked them how long it was since they had sinned with him, and in spite of yourselves, you think that I am the guilty man. This does, naturally, embarras you, when you are in my presence, and at my table. But please ask them, when they come again to confess, how many months or years have passed away since their last love affair with a confessor; and you will see that you may suppose that you are in the house of an honest man. You may look me in the face, and have no fears to address me as if I were still worthy of your esteem; for, thanks be to God, I am not the guilty priest who has ruined and destroyed so many souls here."

The curate had hardly pronounced the last word, when a general "We thank you, for you have taken away a mountain from our shoulders," fell from almost every lip.

"It is a fact that, notwithstanding the good opinion we had of you," said several, "we were in fear that you had missed the right track, and fallen down with your fair penitents, into the ditch."

I felt much relieved; for I was one of those who, in spite of myself, had my secret fears about the honesty of our host. When, very early the next morning, I had begun to hear the confessions, one of those unfortunate victims of the confessor's depravity came to me, and in the midst of many tears and sobs, she told me, with great details, what I repeat here in a few lines:—

"I was only nine years old when my first confessor began to do very criminal things with me, every time I was at his feet confessing my sins. At first, I was ashamed and much disgusted; but soon after, I became so depraved that I was looking eagerly for every opportunity of meeting him, either in his own house, or in the church, in the vestry, and many times, in his own garden, when it was dark at night. That priest did not remain very long; he was removed, to my great regret, to another place, where he died. He was succeeded by another one, who seemed at first to be a very holy man. I made to him a general confession with, it seemed to me, a sincere desire to give up forever, that sinful life; but I fear that my confessions became a cause of sin to that good priest; for, not long after my confession was finished, he declared to me, in the confessional, his love, with such passionate words, that he soon brought me down again into my former criminal habits with him. This lasted six years, when my parents removed to this place. I was very glad for it, for I hoped that, being away from him, I should not be any more a cause of sin to him, and that I might begin a better life. But the fourth time that I went to confess to my new confessor, he invited me to go to his room, where we did things so disgusting together, that I do not know how to confess them. It was two days before my marriage, and the only child I have had is the fruit of that sinful hour. After my marriage, I continued the same criminal life with my confessor. He was the friend of my husband; we had many opportunities of meeting each other, not only when I was going to confess, but when my husband was absent and my child was at school. It was evident to me that several other women were as miserable and criminal as I was myself. This sinful intercourse with my confessor went on, till God Almighty stopped it with a real thunderbolt. My dear only daughter had gone to confess, and received the holy communion. As she came back from church much later than I expected, I inquired the reason which had kept her so long. She then threw herself into my arms, and, with convulsive cries said,—'Dear mother, do not ask me to go to confess any more——Oh! if you could know what my confessor asked me when I was at his feet! and if you could know what he has done with me, and he has forced me to do with him, when he had me alone in his parlor!''

"My poor child could not speak any longer; she fainted in my arms.

"As soon as she recovered, without losing a minute, I dressed myself, and, full of an inexpressible rage, I directed my steps towards the parsonage. But before leaving my house, I had concealed under my shawl a sharp butcher's knife, to stab and kill the villain who had destroyed my dearly beloved child. Fortunately for that priest, God changed my mind before I entered his room: my words to him were few and sharp.

" 'You are a monster!' I said to him. 'Not satisfied to have destroyed me, you want to destroy my own dear child, which is yours also! Shame upon you! I had come with this knife, to put an end to your infamies; but so short a punishment would be too mild a one for such a monster. I want you to live, that you may bear upon your head the curse of the too unsuspecting and unguarded friends whom you have so cruelly deceived and betrayed. I want you to live with the consciousness that you are known by me and many others, as one of the most infamous monsters who has ever defiled this world. But know that if you are not away from this place before the end of this week, I will reveal everything to my husband; and you may be sure that he will not let you live twenty-four hours longer; for he sincerely thinks your daughter is his; he will be the avenger of her honor! I go to denounce you, this very day, to the bishop, that he may take you away from this parish, which you have so shamelessly polluted.'

"The priest threw himself at my feet, and, with tears, asked my pardon, imploring me not to denounce him to the bishop, and promising that he would change his life and begin to live as a good priest. But I remained inexorable. I went to the bishop, and warned his lordship of the sad consequences which would follow, if he kept that curate any longer in this place, as he seemed inclined to do. But before the eight days had expired, he was put at the head of another parish, not very far away from here."

The reader will, perhaps, like to know what has become of this priest.

He remained at the head of that most beautiful parish of Beaumont, as curate, where, I know it for a fact, he continued to destroy his penitents, till a few years before he died, with the reputation of a good priest, an amiable man, and a holy confessor!

For the mystery of iniquity doth already work: . . . .

And then shall that Wicked be revealed, whom the Lord shall consume with the spirit of His mouth, and shall destroy with the brightness of His coming:

Even him, whose coming is after the working of Satan, with all power and signs and lying wonders.

And with all deceivableness of unrighteousness in them that perish; because they received not the love of the truth, that they might be saved.

And for this cause God shall send them strong delusion, that they should believe a lie:

That they all might be damned who believed not the truth, but had pleasure in unrighteousness. (2 Thess. ii. 7—12).

CHAPTER VII

SHOULD AURICULAR CONFESSION BE TOLERATED
AMONG CIVILIZED NATIONS

LET my readers who understand Latin, peruse the extracts I give from Bishop Kenrick, Debreyne, Burchard, Dens, or Liguori, and the most incredulous will learn for themselves that the world, even in the darkest of ages of old paganism, has never seen anything more infamous and degrading as auricular confession.

To say that auricular confession purifies the soul, is not less ridiculous and silly than to say that the white robe of the virgin, or the lily of the valley, will become whiter by being dipped into a bottle of black ink.

Has not the Pope's celibate, by studying his books before he goes to the confessional-box, corrupted his own heart, and plunged his mind, memory, and soul into an atmosphere of impurity which would have been intolerable even to the people of Sodom?

We ask it not only in the name of religion, but of common sense. How can that man, whose heart and memory are just made the reservoir of all the grossest impurities the world has ever known, help others to be chaste and pure?

The idolaters of India believe that they will be purified from their sins by drinking the water with which they have just washed the feet of their priests.

What monstrous doctrine! The souls of men purified by the water which has washed the feet of a miserable, sinful man! Is there any religion more monstrous and diabolical than the Brahmin religion?

Yes, there is one more monstrous, deceitful, and contaminating than that. It is the religion which teaches that the soul of man is purified by a few magical words (called absolution) which come from the lips of a miserable sinner, whose heart and intelligence have just been filled by the unmentionable impurities of Dens, Liguori, Debreyne, Kenrick, &c., &c. For if the poor Indian's soul is not purified by the drinking of the holy (?) water which has touched the feet of his priest, at least that soul cannot be contaminated by it. But who does not clearly see that the drinking of the vile questions of the confessor contaminate, defile and damn the soul?

Who has not been filled with deep compassion and pity for those poor idolaters of Hindoostan, who believe that they will secure to themselves a happy passage to the next life, if they have the good luck to die when holding in their hands the tail of a cow? But there are people among us who are not less worthy of our supreme compassion and pity; for they hope that they will be purified from their sins and be forever happy, if a few magical words (called absolution) fall upon their souls from the polluted lips of a miserable sinner, sent by the Pope of Rome. The dirty tail of a cow, and the magical words of a confessor, to purify the souls and wash away the sins of the world, are equally inventions of the devil. Both religions come from Satan, for they equally substitute the magical power of vile creatures for the blood of Christ, to save the guilty children of Adam. They both ignore that the blood of the Lamb alone cleanseth us from all sin.

Yes! auricular confession is a public act of idolatry. It is asking from a man what God alone, through His Son Jesus, can grant: forgiveness of sins. Has the Saviour of the world ever said to sinners, "Go to this or that man for repentance, pardon and peace?" No: but he has said to all sinners, "Come unto me." And from that day to the end of the world, all the echoes of heaven and earth will repeat these words of the merciful Saviour to all the lost children of Adam—"Come unto me."

When Christ gave to His disciples the power of the keys in these words, "whatsoever ye shall bind on earth, shall be bound in heaven; and whatsoever ye shall loose on earth shall be loosed in heaven" (Matt. xviii. 18), He had just explained His mind by saying, "If thy brother shall trespass against thee" (v. 15). The Son of God Himself, in that solemn hour, protested against the stupendous imposture of Rome, by telling us positively that that power of binding and loosing, forgiving and retaining sins, was only in reference to sins committed against each other. Peter had correctly understood his Master's words, when he asked, "How oft shall my brother sin against me and I forgive him?"

And in order that His true disciples might not be shaken by the sophisms of Rome, or by the glittering nonsense of that band of silly half-Popish Episcopalians, called Tractarians, Ritualists, or Puseyites, the merciful Saviour gave the admirable parable of the poor servant, which He closed by what He has so often repeated, "So likewise shall my Heavenly Father do also unto you, if ye, from your hearts, forgive not every one his brother their trespasses." (Matt. xviii. 35.)

Not long before, He had again mercifully given us His whole mind about the obligation and power which every one of His disciples had of forgiving: "For if ye forgive men their trespasses, your Heavenly Father will also forgive you; but if ye forgive men not their trespasses, neither will your Father forgive your trespasses." (Matt. vi. 14, 15.)

"Be ye therefore merciful as your Father also is merciful; forgive and ye shall be forgiven." (Luke vi. 36, 37.)

Auricular Confession, as the Rev. Dr. Wainwright has so eloquently put it in his "Confession not Auricular," is a diabolical caricature of the forgiveness of sin through the blood of Christ, just as the impious dogma of Transubstantiation is a monstrous caricature of the salvation of the world through His death.

The Romanists, and their ugly tail, the Ritualistic party in the Episcopal Church, make a great noise about the words of our Saviour, in St. John: "Whatsoever sins ye remit, they are remitted unto them: and whatsoever sins ye retain, they are retained." (John xx. 23.)

But again, our Saviour had Himself, once for all, explained what He meant by forgiving and retaining sins—Matt. xviii. 35; Matt. vi. 14, 15; Luke vi. 36, 37.

Nobody but wilfully-blind men could misunderstand Him. Besides that, the Holy Ghost Himself has mercifully taken care that we should not be deceived by the lying traditions of men, on that important subject, when in St. Luke He gave us the explanation of the meaning of John xx. 23, by telling us, "Thus it behoved Christ to suffer, and to rise from the dead the third day: and that repentance and remission of sins should be preached in His name among all nations, beginning at Jerusalem." (Luke xxiv. 46, 47.)

In order that we may better understand the words of our Saviour in St. John xx. 23, let us put them face to face with His own explanations (Luke xxiv. 46, 47.)

LUKE XXIV.

33. And they rose up the same hour and returned to Jerusalem and found the eleven gathered together, and them that were with them.

34. Saying, the Lord is risen indeed, and hath appeared to Simon.

36. And as they thus spake, Jesus himself stood in the midst of them, and said unto them, Peace be unto you.

37. But they were terrified and affrighted, and supposed that they had seen a spirit.

38. And he said unto them, Why are ye troubled? and why do thoughts arise in your hearts?

39. Behold my hands and my feet, that it is I myself: handle me, and see; for a spirit hath not flesh and bones as ye see me have.

40. And when he had thus spoken, he showed them his hands and his feet.

JOHN XX.

18. Mary Magdalene came and told the disciples that she had seen the Lord, and that he had spoken these things unto her.

19. Then the same day at evening, being the first day of the week, when the doors were shut where the disciples were assembled, for fear of the Jews, came Jesus and stood in the midst, and saith unto them, Peace be unto you.

20. And when he had so said, he shewed unto them his hands and his side. Then were the disciples glad, when they saw the Lord.

41. And while they yet believed not for joy, and wondered, he said unto them, Have ye here any meat?

42. And they gave him a piece of a broiled fish, and of an honeycomb.

43. And he took it, and did eat before them.

44. And he said unto them, These are the words which I spoke unto you, while I was yet with you, that all things must be fulfilled, which were written in the law of Moses, and in the prophets, and in the psalms concerning me.

45. Then opened he their understanding, that they might understand the Scriptures,

46. And said unto them, Thus it is written, and thus it behoved Christ to suffer, and to rise from the dead the third day.

47. And that repentance and remission of sins should be preached in his name among all nations, beginning at Jerusalem.

21. Then said Jesus to them again, Peace be unto you: as my Father hath sent me, even so send I you.

22. And when he had said this, he breathed on them, and saith unto them, Receive ye the Holy Ghost:

23. Whose soever sins ye remit, they are remitted unto them; whose soever sins ye retain, they are retained.

Three things are evident from comparing the report of St. John and St. Luke:—

1. They speak of the same event, though one of them gives certain details omitted by the other, as we find in the rest of the gospels.

2. The words of St. John, "Whose soever sins ye remit, they are remitted unto them; and whose soever sins ye retain, they are retained," are explained by the Holy Ghost Himself, in St. Luke, as meaning that the apostles shall preach repentance and forgiveness of sins through Christ. It is just what our Saviour has Himself said in St. Matthew ix. 13: "But go ye and learn what that meaneth, I will have mercy, and not sacrifice: for I am not come to call the righteous, but sinners to repentance."

It is just the same doctrine taught by Peter (Acts ii. 38): "Then Peter said unto them, Repent, and be baptized every one of you in the name of Jesus Christ for the remission of sins, and ye shall receive the gift of the Holy Ghost."

Just the same doctrine of the forgiveness of sins not through auricular confession or absolution but through the preaching of the Word: "Be it known unto you therefore, men and brethren, that through this man is preached unto you the forgiveness of sins" (Acts xiii. 38).

3. The third thing which is evident is that the apostles were not alone when Christ appeared and spoke, but that several of His other disciples, even some women, were there.

If the Romanists, then, could prove that Christ established auricular confession, and gave the power of absolution, by what He said in that solemn hour, women as well as men—in fact, every believer in Christ—would be authorized to hear confessions and give absolution. The Holy Ghost was not promised or given only to the Apostles, but to every believer, as we see in Acts i. 15, and ii. 1, 2, 3.

But the Gospel of Christ, as well as the history of the first ten centuries of Christianity, is the witness that auricular confession and absolution are nothing else but a sacrilegious as well as a most stupendous imposture.

What tremendous efforts the priests of Rome have made, these last five centuries, and are still making, to persuade their dupes that the Son of God was making of them a privileged caste, a caste endowed with the Divine and exclusive power of opening and shutting the gates of Heaven, when He said, "Whatsoever ye shall bind on earth, shall be bound in Heaven; and whatsoever ye shall loose on earth shall be loosed in Heaven."

But our adorable Saviour, who perfectly foresaw those diabolical efforts on the part of the priests of Rome, entirely upset every vestige of their foundation by saying immediately, "Again I say unto you, That if two of you shall agree on earth as touching any thing that they shall ask, it shall be done for them of my Father which is in Heaven. For where two or three are gathered together in My name, there am I in the midst of them" (Matt. xviii. 19, 20.)

Would the priests of Rome attempt to make us believe that these words of the 19th and 20th verses are addressed to them exclusively? They have not yet dared to say it. They confess that these words are addressed to all His disciples. But our Saviour positively says that the other words, implicating the so-called power of the priests to hear the confession and give the absolution, are addressed to the very same persons—"I say unto you," &c., &c. The you of the 19th and 20th verses is the same you of the 18th. The power of loosing and unloosing is, then, given to all—those who would be offended and would forgive. Then, our Saviour had not in His mind to form a caste of men with any marvellous power over the rest of His disciples. The priests of Rome, then, are impostors, and nothing else, when they say that the power of loosing and unloosing sins was exclusively granted to them.

Instead of going to the confessor, let the Christian go to his merciful God, through Christ, and say, "Forgive us our trespasses as we forgive them that trespass against us." This is the Truth, not as it comes from the Vatican, but as it comes from Calvary, where our debts were paid, with the only condition that we should believe, repent and love.

Have not the Popes publicly and repeatedly anathematized the sacred principle of Liberty of Conscience? Have they not boldly said, in the teeth of the nations of Europe, that Liberty of Conscience must be destroyed—killed at any cost? Has not the whole world heard the sentence of death to liberty coming from the lips of the old man of the Vatican? But where is the scaffold on which the doomed Liberty must perish? That scaffold is the confessional-box. Yes, in the confessional, the Pope has his 100,000 high executioners! There they are, day and night, with sharp daggers in hand, stabbing Liberty to the heart.

In vain will noble France expel her old tyrants in order to be free; in vain will she shed the purest blood of her heart to protect and save liberty! True liberty cannot live a day there so long as the executioners of the Pope are free to stab her on their 100,000 scaffolds.

In vain chivalrous Spain will call Liberty to give a new life to her people. Liberty cannot set her feet there, except to die, so long as the Pope is allowed to strike her in his 50,000 confessionals.

And free America, too, will see all her so dearly-bought liberties destroyed, the day that the confessional-box is universally reared in her midst.

Auricular Confession and Liberty cannot stand together on the same ground; either one or the other must fall.

Liberty must sweep away the confessional, as she has swept away the demon of slavery, or she is doomed to perish.

Can a man be free in his own house, so long as there is another who has the legal right to spy all his actions, and direct not only every step, but every thought of his wife and children? Can that man boast of a home whose wife and children are under the control of another? Is not that unfortunate man really the slave of the ruler and master of his household? And when a whole nation is composed of such husbands and fathers, is it not a nation of abject, degraded slaves?

To a thinking man, one of the most strange phenomena is that our modern nations allow their most sacred rights to be trampled under foot, and destroyed by the Papacy, the sworn enemy of Liberty, through a mistaken respect and love for that same Liberty!

No people have more respect for Liberty of Conscience than the Americans; but has the noble State of Illinois allowed Joe Smith and Brigham Young to degrade and enslave the American women under the pretext of Liberty of Conscience, appealed to by the so-called "Latter-day Saints?" No! The ground was soon made too hot for the tender conscience of the modern prophets. Joe Smith perished when attempting to keep his captive wives in his chains, and Brigham Young had to fly to the solitudes of the Far West, to enjoy what he called his liberty of conscience with the thirty women whom he had degraded, and enchained under his yoke. But even in that remote solitude the false prophet has heard the distant peals of the roaring thunder. The threatened voice of the great Republic has troubled his rest, and before his death he wisely spoke of going as much as possible out of the reach of Christian civilization, before the dark and threatening clouds which he saw on the horizon would hurl upon him their irresistible storms.

Will any one blame the American people for so going to the rescue of women? No, surely not.

But what is this confessional box? Nothing but a citadel and stronghold of Mormonism.

What is this Father Confessor, with few exceptions, but a lucky Brigham Young?

I do not want to be believed on my ipse dixit. What I ask from serious thinkers is, that they should read the encyclicals of the Piuses, the Gregorys, the Benoits, and many other Popes, "De Sollicitantibus." There they will see, with their own eyes, that, as a general thing, the confessor has more women to serve him than the Mormon prophets ever had. Let him read the memoirs of one of the most venerable men of the Church of Rome, Bishop Scipio de Ricci, and they will see, with their own eyes, that the confessors are more free with their penitents, even nuns, than husbands are with their wives. Let them hear the testimony of one of the noblest princesses of Italy, Henrietta Carracciolo, who still lives, and they will know that the Mormons have more respect for women than the greater part of the confessors have. Let them read the personal experience of Miss O'Gorman, five years a nun in the United States, and they will understand that the priests and their female penitents, even nuns, are out-raging all the laws of God and man, through the dark mysteries of auricular confession. That Miss O'Gorman, as well as Miss Henrietta Carraccioli, are still living. Why are they not consulted by those who like to know the truth, and who fear that we exaggerate the infamies which come from "auricular confession" as from their infallible source? Let them hear the lamentations of Cardinal Baronius, St. Bernard, Savanarola, Pius, Gregory, St. Therese, St. Liguori, on the unspeakable and irreparable ruin spread all along the ways and all over the countries haunted by the Pope's confessors, and they will know that the confessional-box is the daily witness of abominations which would hardly have been tolerated in the lands of Sodom and Gomorrah. Let the legislators, the fathers and husbands of every nation and tongue, interrogate Father Gavazzi, Grassi, and thousands of living priests who, like myself, have miraculously been taken out from that Egyptian servitude to the promised land, and they will tell you the same old, old story—that the confessional-box is for the greatest part of the confessors and female penitents, a real pit of perdition, into which they promiscuously fall and perish. Yes; they will tell you that the soul and heart of your wife and daughter are purified by the magical words of the confessional, just as the souls of the poor idolaters of Hindoostan are purified by the tail of the cow which they hold in their hands, when they died. Study the pages of the past history of England, France, Italy, Spain, &c., &c., and you will see that the gravest and most reliable historians have, everywhere, found mysteries of iniquity in the confessional-box which their pen refused to trace.

In the presence of such public, undeniable, and lamentable facts, have not the civilized nations a duty to perform? Is it not time that the children of light, the true disciples of the Gospel, all over the world, should rally round the banners of Christ, and go, shoulder to shoulder, to the rescue of women?

Woman is to society what the roots are to the most precious trees of your orchard. If you knew that a thousand worms are biting the roots of those noble trees, that their leaves are already fading away, their rich fruits, though yet unripe, are falling on the ground, would you not unearth the roots and sweep away the worms?

The confessor is the worm which is biting, polluting, and destroying the very roots of civil and religious society, by contaminating, debasing, and enslaving woman.

Before the nations can see the reign of peace, happiness, and liberty, which Christ has promised, they must, like the Israelites, pull down the walls of Jericho. The confessional is the modern Jericho, which defiantly dares the children of God!

Let, then, the people of the Lord, the true soldiers of Christ, rise up and rally around His banners; and let them fearlessly march, shoulder to shoulder, on the doomed city: let the trumpets of Israel be sounded around its walls: let fervent prayers go to the throne of Mercy, from the heart of every one for whom the Lamb has been slain: let such a unanimous cry of indignation be heard, through the length and breadth of the land, against that greatest and most monstrous imposture of modern times, that the earth will tremble under the feet of the confessor, so that his very knees will shake, and soon the walls of Jericho will fall, the confessional will disappear, and its unspeakable pollutions will no more imperil the very existence of society.

Then the multitudes who were kept captive will come to the Lamb, who will make them pure with His blood and free with His word.

Then the redeemed nations will sing a song of joy: "Babylon, the great, the mother of harlots and abominations of the earth, is fallen! is fallen!"

CHAPTER VIII

DOES AURICULAR CONFESSION BRING PEACE
TO THE SOUL?

THE connecting of Peace with Auricular Confession is surely the most cruel sarcasm ever uttered in human language.

It would be less ridiculous and false to admire the calmness of the sea, and the stillness of the atmosphere, when a furious storm raises the foaming waves to the sky, than to speak of the Peace of the soul either during or after the confession.

I know it; the confessors and their dupes chorus every tune by crying "Peace, peace!" But the God of truth and holiness answers, "There is no peace for the wicked!"

The fact is, that no human words can adequately express the anxieties of the soul before confession, its unspeakable confusion in the act of confessing, or its deadly terrors after confession.

Let those who have never drunk of the bitter waters which flow from the confessional box, read the following plain and correct recital of my own first experience in auricular confession. They are nothing less than the history of what nine-tenths of the penitents* of Rome, old and young, are subject to; and they will know what to think of that marvelous Peace about which Romanists, and their silly copyists, the Ritualists, have written so many eloquent lies.

In the year 1819, my parents had sent me from Murray Bay (La Mal Baie), where they lived, to an excellent school at St. Thomas. I was then about nine years old. I boarded with an uncle, who, though a nominal Roman Catholic, did not believe a word of what his priest preached. But my aunt had the reputation of being a very devoted woman. Our schoolmaster, Mr. John Jones, was a well-educated Englishman, and a staunch PROTESTANT. This last circumstance had excited the wrath of the Roman Catholic priest against the teacher and his numerous pupils to such an extent, that they were often denounced from the pulpit with very hard words. But if he did not like us, I must admit that we were paying him with his own coin.

But let us come to my first lesson in Auricular Confession. No! No words can express to those who have never had any experience in the matter, the consternation, anxiety and shame of a poor Romish child, when he hears his priest saying from the pulpit, in a grave and solemn tone: "This week you will send your children to confession. Make them understand that this action is one of the most important of their lives, that for every

---

* By the word *penitents*, Rome means not those who *repent*, but those who *confess* to the priest.

one of them it will decide their eternal happiness or ruin. Fathers, mothers and guardians of those children, if, through your fault or theirs, your children are guilty of a false confession: if they do not confess everything to the priest who holds the place of God Himself, this sin is often irreparable: the devil will take possession of their hearts, they will lie to their father confessor, or rather to Jesus Christ, of whom he is the representative: their lives will be a series of sacrileges, their death and eternity those of reprobates. Teach them, therefore, to examine thoroughly all their actions, words, thoughts and desires, in order to confess everything just as it occurred, without any disguise."

I was in the Church of St. Thomas, when these words fell upon me like a thunderbolt. I had often heard my mother say, when at home, and my aunt, since I had come to St. Thomas, that upon the first confession depended my eternal happiness or misery. That week was, therefore, to decide the vital question of my eternity!

Pale and dismayed, I left the Church after the service, and returned to the house of my relations. I took my place at the table, but could not eat, so much was I troubled. I went to my room for the purpose of commencing my examination of conscience, and to try to recall every one of my sinful actions, thoughts and words!

Although scarcely over nine years of age, this task was really overwhelming to me. I knelt down to pray to the Virgin Mary for help, but I was so much taken up with the fear of forgetting something or making a bad confession, that I muttered my prayers without the least attention to what I said. It became still worse, when I commenced counting my sins; my memory, though very good, became confused; my head grew dizzy; my heart beat with a rapidity which exhausted me, my brow was covered with perspiration. After a considerable length of time spent in these painful efforts, I felt bordering on despair from the fear that it was impossible for me to remember exactly everything, and to confess each sin as it occurred. The night following was almost a sleepless one; and when sleep did come, it could hardly be called sleep, but a suffocating delirium. In a frightful dream, I felt as if I had been cast into hell, for not having confessed all my sins to the priest. In the morning I awoke fatigued and prostrate by the phantoms and emotions of that terrible night. In similar troubles of mind were passed the three days which preceded my first confession.

I had constantly before me the countenance of that stern priest who had never smiled on me. He was present to my thoughts during the days, and in my dreams during the nights, as the minister of an angry God, justly irritated against me on account of my sins. Forgiveness had indeed been promised to me, on condition of a good confession; but my place had also been shown to me in hell, if my confession was not as near perfection as possible.

Now, my troubled conscience told me that there were ninety chances against one that my confession would be bad, either if by my own fault, I forgot some sins, or if I was without that contrition of which I had heard so much, but the nature and affects of which were a perfect chaos in my mind.

At length came the day of my confession, or rather of judgment and condemnation. I presented myself to the priest, the Rev. Mr. Beaubien.

He had, then, the defects of lisping or stammering, which we often turned into ridicule. And, as nature had unfortunately endowed me with admirable powers as a mimic, the infirmities of this poor priest afforded only too good an opportunity for the exercise of my talent. Not only was it one of my favorite amusements to imitate him before the pupils amidst roars of laughter, but also, I preached portions of his sermons before his parishioners with similar results. Indeed, many of them came from considerable distances to enjoy the opportunity of listening to me, and they, more than once, rewarded me with cakes of maple sugar for my performances.

These acts of mimicry were, of course, among my sins; and it became necessary for me to examine myself upon the number of times I had mocked the priests. This circumstance was not calculated to make my confession easier or more agreeable.

At last, the dread moment arrived, I knelt for the first time at the side of my confessor, but my whole frame trembled: I repeated the prayer preparatory to confession, scarcely knowing what I said, so much was I troubled by fears.

By the instructions which had been given us before confession, we had been made to believe that the priest was the true representative, yea, almost the personification of Jesus Christ. The consequence was that I believed my greatest sin was that of mocking the priest—and I, as I had been told that it was proper first to confess the greatest sins, I commenced thus: "Father, I accuse myself of having mocked a priest!"

Hardly had I uttered these words, "mocked a priest," when this pretended representative of the humble Jesus, turning towards me, and looking in my face, in order to know me better, asked abruptly: "What priest did you mock, my boy?"

I would have rather chosen to cut out my tongue than to tell him, to his face, who it was. I, therefore, kept silent for a while; but my silence made him very nervous, and almost angry. With a haughty tone of voice, he said: "What priest did you take the liberty of thus mocking, my boy?" I saw that I had to answer. Happily, his haughtiness had made me bolder and firmer; I said: "Sir, you are the priest whom I mocked!"

"But how many times did you take upon yourself to mock me, my boy?" asked he, angrily.

"I tried to find out the number of times, but I never could."

"You must tell me how many times; for to mock one's own priest is a great sin."

"It is impossible for me to give you the number of times," I answered.

Well, my child, I will help your memory by asking you questions. Tell me the truth. Do you think you mocked me ten times?"

"A great many times more," I answered.

"Have you mocked me fifty times?"

"Oh! many more still!"

"A hundred times?"

"Say five hundred, and perhaps more," I answered.

"Well, my boy, do you spend all your time in mocking me?"

"Not all my time; but, unfortunately, I have done it very often."

"Yes, you may well say 'unfortunately!' for to mock your priest, who holds the place of our Lord Jesus Christ, is a great sin and a great misfortune for you. But tell me, my little boy, what reason have you for mocking me thus?"

In my examination of conscience, I had not foreseen that I should be obliged to give the reasons for mocking the priest, and I was thunderstruck by his questions. I dared not answer, and I remained for a long time dumb, from the shame that overpowered me. But, with a harrassing perseverance, the priest insisted upon my telling why I had mocked him; assuring me that I would be damned if I did not speak the whole truth. So I decided to speak, and said: "I mocked you for several things."

"What made you first mock me?" asked the priest.

"I laughed at you because you lisp: among the pupils of the school, and other people, it often happens that we imitate your preaching to laugh at you," I answered.

"For what other reason did you laugh at me, my little boy?"

For a long time I was silent. Every time I opened my mouth to speak, my courage failed me. But the priest continued to urge me; I said at last: "It is rumored in town that you love the girls: that you visit the Misses Richards almost every night; and this made us laugh often."

The poor priest was evidently overwhelmed by my answer, and ceased questioning me on that subject. Changing the conversation, he said: "What are your other sins?"

I began to confess them according to the order in which they came to my memory. But the feeling of shame which overpowered me, in repeating all my sins to that man, was a thousand times greater than that of having offended God. In reality, this feeling of human shame, which absorbed my thoughts, nay, my whole being, left no room for any religious feeling at all, and I am certain that this is the case with more than the greater part of those who confess their sins to the priest.

When I had confessed all the sins I could remember, the priest began to put to me the strangest questions about matters upon which my pen must be silent . . . I replied, "Father, I do not understand what you ask me."

"I question you," he answered, "on the sins of the sixth commandment of God (seventh in the Bible). Do confess all, my little boy, for you will go to hell, if, through your fault, you omit anything."

And thereupon he dragged my thoughts into regions of iniquity which, thanks be to God, had hitherto been quite unknown to me.

I answered him again, "I do not understand you," or "I have never done those wicked things."

Then, skilfully shifting to some secondary matters, he would soon slyly and cunningly come back to his favorite subject, namely, sins of licentiousness.

His questions were so unclean that I blushed, and felt nauseated with disgust and shame. More than once, I had been, to my great regret, in the company of bad boys, but not one of them had offended my moral nature so much as this priest had done. Not one of them had ever approached the shadow of the things from which that man tore the veil, and which he placed before the eyes of my soul. In vain I told him that I was not guilty of those things; that I did not even understand what he asked me; but he would not let me off.

Like a vulture bent upon tearing the poor defenceless bird that falls into its claws, that cruel priest seemed determined to ruin and defile my heart.

At last he asked me a question in a form of expression so bad, that I was really pained and put beside myself. I felt as if I had received the shock from an electric battery: a feeling of horror made me shudder. I was filled with such indignation that, speaking loud enough to be heard by many, I told him: "Sir, I am very wicked, but I was never guilty of what you mention to me: please don't ask me any more of those questions, which will teach me more wickedness than I ever knew."

The remainder of my confession was short. The stern rebuke I had given him had evidently made the priest blush, if it had not frightened him. He stopped short, and gave me some very good advice, which might have done me good, if the deep wounds which his questions had inflicted upon my soul, had not so absorbed my thoughts as to prevent me giving attention to what he said. He gave me a short penance and dismissed me.

I left the confessional irritated and confused. From the shame of what I had just heard, I dared not raise my eyes from the ground. I went into a corner of the church to do my penance, that is to recite the prayers which he had indicated to me. I remained for a long time in the church. I had need of calm, after the terrible trial through which I had just passed. But vainly I sought for rest. The shameful questions which had just been asked me; the new world of iniquity into which I had been introduced; the impure phantoms by which my childish head had been defiled, confused and troubled my mind so much, that I began to weep bitterly.

I left the church only when forced to do so by the shades of night, and came back to my uncle's house with a feeling of shame and uneasiness, as if I had done a bad action and feared lest I should be detected. My trouble was much increased when my uncle jestingly said: "Now that you have been to confess, you will be a good boy. But if you are not a better boy, you will be a more learned one, if your confessor has taught you what mine did when I confessed for the first time."

I blushed and remained silent. My aunt said:

"You must feel happy, now that you have made your confession: do you not?"

I gave an evasive answer, but could not entirely conceal the confusion which overwhelmed me. I went to bed early; but I could hardly sleep.

I thought I was the only boy whom the priest had asked these polluting questions; but great was my confusion, when, on going to school the next day, I learned that my companions had not been happier than I had been. The only difference was that, instead of being grieved as I was, they laughed at it.

"Did the priest ask you this and that," they would demand, laughing boisterously; I refused to reply, and said: "Are you not ashamed to speak of these things?"

"Ah! ah! how scrupulous you are," continued they, "if it is not a sin for the priest to speak to us on these matters, how can it be a sin for us to laugh at it." I felt confounded, not knowing what to answer. But my confusion increased not a little when soon after, I perceived that the young girls of the school had not been less polluted or scandalized than the boys. Although keeping at a sufficient distance from us to prevent us from understanding everything they had to say on their confessional experience, those girls were sufficiently near to let us hear many things which it would have been better for us not to know. Some of them seemed thoughtful, sad, and shameful; but some of them laughed heartily at what they had learned in the confessional-box.

I was very indignant against the priest; and thought in my-self that he was a very wicked man for having put to us such repelling questions. But I was wrong. That priest was honest; he was only doing his duty, as I have known since, when study-ing the theologians of Rome. The Rev. Mr. Beaubien was a real gentleman; and if he had been free to follow the dictates of his honest conscience, it is my strong conviction, he would never have sullied our young hearts with such impure ideas. But what has the honest conscience of a priest to do in the confessional, except to be silent and dumb; the priest of Rome is an automaton, tied to the feet of the Pope by an iron chain. He can move, go right or left, up or down; he can think and act, but only at the bidding of the infallible god of Rome. The priest knows the will of his modern divinity only through his approved emissaries, ambassadors, and theologians. With shame on my brow, and bitter tears of regret flowing just now, on my cheeks, I confess that I have had myself to learn by heart those damning ques-tions, and put them to the young and the old who like me, were fed with the diabolical doctrines of the Church of Rome, in refer-ence to auricular confession.

Some time after, some people waylaid and whipped that very same priest, when, during a very dark night he was coming back from visiting his fair young penitents, the Misses Richards. And the next day, the conspirators having met at the house of Dr. Stephen Tache, to give a report of what they had done to the half secret society to which they belonged, I was invited by my young friend Louis Cazault* to conceal myself with him, in an adjoining room, where we could hear everything without being seen. I find in the old manuscripts of "my young years' recollec-tions" the following address of Mr. Dubord, one of the principal merchants of St. Thomas:

"Mr. President,—I was not among those who gave to the priest the expression of the public feelings with the eloquent

* He died many years after when at the head of the Laval University

voice of the whip, but I wish I had been; I would heartily have co-operated to give that so well-deserved lesson to the father confessors of Canada; and let me give you my reasons for that.

"My child, who is hardly twelve years old, went to confess, as did the other girls of the village, some time ago. It was against my will. I know by my own experience, that of all actions, confession is the most degrading of a person's life. I can imagine nothing so well calculated to destroy forever one's self-respect, as the modern invention of the confessional. Now, what is a person without self-respect? Especially a woman? Is not all forever lost without this?

"In the confessional, everything is corruption of the lowest grade. There the girls' thoughts, lips, hearts and souls are forever polluted. Do I need to prove you this! No! for though you have long since given up auricular confession, as below the dignity of man, you have not forgotten the lessons of corruption which you have received from it. Those lessons have remained on your souls as the scars left by the red-hot iron upon the brow of the slave, to be a perpetual witness of his slavery, to be a perpetual witness of his shame and servitude.

"The confessional-box is the place where our wives and daughters learn things which would make the most degraded women of our cities blush!

"Why are all Roman Catholic nations inferior to nations belonging to Protestantism? Only in the confessional can the solution of that problem be found. And why are Roman Catholic nations degraded in proportion to their submission to their priests? It is because the more often the individuals composing those nations go to confess, the more rapidly they sink in the sphere of intelligence and morality. A terrible example of the auricular confession depravity has just occurred in my own family.

"As I have said a moment ago, I was against my own daughter going to confession, but her poor mother, who is under the control of the priest, earnestly wanted her to go. Not to have a disagreeable scene in my house, I had to yield to the tears of my wife.

"On the following day of the confesion, they believed I was absent, but I was in my office, with the door sufficiently opened to hear everything which could be said by my wife and the child. And the following conversation took place:

" 'What makes you so thoughtful and sad, my dear Lucy, since you went to confess? It seems to me you should feel happier since you had the privilege of confessing your sins.'

"My child answered not a word; she remained absolutely silent.

"After two or three minutes of silence, I heard the mother saying: 'Why do you weep, my dear Lucy? are you sick?'

"But no answer yet from the child!"

"You may well suppose that I was all attention: I had my secret suspicions about the dreadful mystery which had taken place. My heart throbbed with uneasiness and anger.

"After a short silence, my wife spoke again to her child, but with sufficient firmness to decide her to answer at last. In a trembling voice, she said:

" 'Oh! dear mamma, if you knew what the priest has asked me, and what he said to me when I confessed, you would perhaps be as sad as I am.'

" 'But what can he have said to you? He is a holy man, you must have misunderstood him, if you think that he has said anything wrong.'

"My child threw herself in her mother's arms, and answered with a voice, half suffocated with her sobs: 'Do not ask me to tell you what the priest has said—it is so shameful that I cannot repeat it—his words have stuck to my heart as the leech put to the arm of my little friend, the other day.'

" 'What does the priest think of me, for having put me such questions?'

"My wife answered: 'I will go to the priest and will teach him a lesson. I have noticed myself that he goes too far when questioning old people, but I had the hope he was more prudent with children. I ask of you, however, never to speak of this to anybody, especially let not your poor father know anything about it, for he has little enough of religion already, and this would leave him without any at all.'

"I could not refrain myself any longer: I abruptly entered the parlor. My daughter threw herself into my arms; my wife screamed with terror, and almost fell into a swoon. I said to my child: 'If you love me, put your hand on my heart, and promise never to go again to confess. Fear God, my child, love Him, and walk in His presence. For His eyes see you everywhere. Remember that He is always ready to forgive and bless you every time you turn your heart to Him. Never place yourself again at the feet of a priest, to be defiled and degraded.'

"This my daughter promised to me.

"When my wife had recovered from her surprise, I said to her:—

" 'Madame, it is long since the priest became everything, and your husband nothing, to you! There is a hidden and terrible power which governs you; it is the power of the priest; this you have often denied, but it can not be denied any longer; the Providence of God has decided to-day that this power should be destroyed forever in my house; I want to be the only ruler of my family; from this moment, the power of the priest over you is forever abolished. Whenever you go and take your heart and your secrets to the feet of the priest, be so kind as not to come back any more into my house as my wife.' "

This is one of the thousands of specimens of the peace of conscience brought to the soul through auricular confession. If it were my intention to publish a treatise on this subject, I could give many similar instances, but as I only desire to write a short chapter, I will adduce but one other fact to show the awful deception practised by the Church of Rome, when she invites persons to come to confession, under the pretext that peace to the soul will be the reward of their obedience. Let us hear the testimony of another living and unimpeachable witness, about this peace of the soul, before, during, and after auricular confession. In her remarkable book, "Personal Experience of Roman Catholicism," Miss Eliza Richardson writes (pages 34 and 35) :—*

"Thus I silenced my foolish quibbling, and went on to test of a convert's fervor and sincerity in confession. And, here, was assuredly a fresh source of pain and disquiet, and one not so easily vanquished. The theory had appeared, as a whole, fair and rational; but the reality, in some of its details was terrible!

"Divested, for the public gaze, of its darkest ingredients, and dressed up, in their theological works, in false and meretricious pretensions to truth and purity, it exhibited a dogma only calculated to exact a beneficial influence on mankind, and to prove a source of morality and usefulness. But oh, as with all ideals, how unlike was the actual?

"Here, however, I may remark, in passing, the effect produced upon my mind by the first sight of the older editions of 'the Garden of the Soul.' I remember the stumbling-block it was to me; my sense of womanly delicacy was shocked. It was a dark page in my experience when I first knelt at the feet of a mortal man to confess what should have been poured into the ear of God alone. I cannot dwell upon this . . . . Though I believe my confessor was, on the whole, as guarded as his manners were kind, at some things I was strangely startled, utterly confounded.

"The purity of mind and delicacy in which I had been nurtured, had not prepared me for such an ordeal; and my own sincerity, and dread of committing a sacrilege, tended to augment

---

* This Miss Richardson is a well-known Protestant lady, in England, who turned Romanist, became a nun, and returned to her Protestant church, after five years' personal experience of Popery. She is still living as an unimpeachable witness of the depravity of auricular confession.

the painfulness of the occasion. One circumstance, especially, I will recall, which my fettered conscience persuaded me I was obliged to name. My distress and terror, doubtless, made me less explicit than I otherwise might have been. The questioning, however, it elicited, and the ideas supplied by it, outraged my feelings to such an extent, that, forgetting all respect for my confessor, and careless, even, at the moment, whether I received absolution or not, I hastily exclaimed, 'I cannot say a word more, while the thought rushed into my mind, 'all is true that their enemies say of them.' Here, however, prudence dictated to my questioner to put the matter no further; and the kind and almost respectful tone he immediately assumed, went far towards effacing an impression so injurious. On rising from my knees, when I should have gladly fled to any distance rather than have encountered his gaze, he addressed me in the most familiar manner on different subjects, and detained me some time in talking. What share I took in the conversation I never knew, and all that I remember, was by burning cheeks, and inability to raise my eyes from the ground.

"Here I would not be supposed to be intentionally casting a stigma upon an individual. Nor am I throwing unqualified blame upon the priesthood. It is the system which is at fault, a system which teaches that things, even at the remembrance of which degraded humanity must blush in the presence of heaven and its angels, should be laid open, dwelt upon, and exposed in detail to the sullied ears of a corrupt and fallen fellow-mortal, who, of like passions with the penitent at his feet, is thereby exposed to temptations the most dark and dangerous. But what shall we say of woman? Draw a veil! Oh purity, modesty! and every womanly feeling! a veil as oblivion, over the fearfully dangerous experience thou art called to pass through!" (Pages 37 and 38.)

"Ah! there are things which cannot be recorded! facts too startling, and at the same time too delicately intricate, to admit a public portrayal, to meet the public gaze; but the cheek can blush in secret at the true images which memory evokes, and the oppressed mind shrinks back in horror from the dark shadows which have saddened and overwhelmed it. I appeal to converts to converts of the gentler sex, and ask them, fearlessly ask them what was the first impression made on your minds and feelings by the confessional? I do not ask how subsequent familiarization has weakened the effects; but when acquaintance was first made with it, how were you affected by it? I was not the impure, the already defiled, for to such it is sadly susceptible of being made a darker source of guilt and shame; I appeal to the pure minded and delicate, the pure in heart and sentiment. Was not your first impression one of inexpressible dread and bewilderment followed by a sense of humiliation and degradation not easily to be defined or supported?" (Page 39.) "The memory of that time (first auricular confession) will ever be painful and abhorrent to me; though subsequent experience has thrown even that far into the background. It was my initiatory lesson upon subjects which ought never to enter the imagination of girlhood; my introduction into a region which ought never to be approached by the guileless and the pure." (Page 61.) "One or two individuals (Roman Catholics) soon formed a close intimacy with me, and discoursed with a freedom and plainness I had never before encountered. My acquaintances, however, had been brought up in convents, or familiar with them for years, and I could not gainsay their statement.

"I was reluctant to believe more than I had experienced. The proof, however, was destined to come in no dubious shape at no distant day . . . . A dark and sullied page of experience was fast opening upon me; but so unaccustomed was the eye which scanned it, that I could scarcely at all, at once, believe in its truth! And it was of hypocrisy so hateful, of sacrilege so terrible, and abuse so gross of all things pure and holy, and in the person of one bound by his vows, his position, and every law of his Church, as well as of God, to set a high example, that, for a time, all confidence in the very existence of sincerity and goodness was in danger of being shaken; sacraments, deemed the most sacred, were profaned; vows disregarded, vaunted secrecy of the confessional covertly infringed, and its sanctity abused to an unhallowed purpose; while even private visitation was converted into a channel for temptation, and made the occasion of unholy freedom of words and manner. So ran the account of evil, and a dire account it was. By it all serious thoughts of religion were well nigh extinguished. The influence was fearful and polluting, the whirl of excitement inexpressible; I cannot enter into minute particulars here, every sense of feminine delicacy and womanly feeling shrink from such a task. This much, however, I can say, that I, in conjunction with two other young friends, took a journey to a confessor, an inmate of a religious house, who lived at some distance, to lay the affair before him, thinking that he would take some remedial measures adequate to the urgency of the case. He heard our united statements, expressed great indignation, and at once commanded us each to write and detail the circumstances of the case to the Bishop of the district. This we did, but of course never heard the result. The reminiscences of these dreary and wretched months seem now like some hideous and guilty dream. It was actual familiarization with unholiest things!" (Page 63.)

"The Romish religion teaches that if you omit to name anything in confession, however repugnant or revolting to purity, which you even doubt having committed, your subsequent confessions are thus rendered null and sacrilegious; whilst it also inculcates that sins of thought should be confessed in order that the confessor may judge of their mortal or venial character. What sort of a chain this links around the strictly conscientious, I would attempt to portray if I could. But it must have been worn to understand its torturing character! Suffice it to say that, for months past, according to this standard, I had not made a good confession at all! And now, filled with remorse for my past sacrilegious sinfulness, I resolved on making a new general confession to the religieux alluded to. But this confessor's scrupulosity exceeded everything I had hitherto encountered. He told me some things were mortal sins which I had never before imagined could be such, and thus threw so many fetters around my conscience, that a host of anxieties for my first general confession was awakened within me. I had no resource, then, but to re-make that, and thus I afresh entered on the bitter path I had deemed I should never have occasion again to tread. But if my first confession had lacerated my feelings, what was it to this one? Words have no power, language has no expression to characterise the emotion that marked it!

"The difficulty I felt in making a full and explicit avowal of all that distressed me, furnished my confessor with a plea for his assistance in the questioning department, and fain would I conceal much of what passed then as a foul blot on my memory. I soon found that he made mortal sins of what my first confessor had professed to treat but lightly, and he did not scruple to say that I had never yet made a good confession at all. My ideas, therefore, became more complicated and confused as I proceeded, until, at length, I began to feel doubtful of ever accomplishing my task in any degree satisfactorily; and my mind and memory were positively racked to recall every iota of every kind, real or imaginary, that might if omitted, hereafter be occasion of uneasiness. Things, heretofore held comparatively trifling, were recounted, and pronounced damnable sins; and as, day after day, I knelt at the feet of that man, answering questions and listening to admonitions calculated to bow my very soul to the dust, I felt as though I should hardly be able to raise my head again!" (Page 63.)

This is the peace which flows from auricular confession! I solemnly declare that, except in a few cases, in which the confidence of the penitents is bordering on idiocy, or in which they have been transformed into immoral brutes, nine tenths of the multitudes who go to confess are obliged to recount some such desolate narrative as that of Miss Richardson, when they are sufficiently honest to say the truth.

The most fanatical apostles of auricular confession cannot deny that the examination of conscience, which must precede confession, is a most difficult task, a task which, instead of filling the mind with peace, fills it with anxiety and serious fears. Is it then only after confession that they promise such peace? But they know very well that this promise is also a cruel deception . . . for to make a good confession the penitent has to relate not only all his bad actions, but all his bad thoughts and desires, their number and various aggravating circumstances. But have they found a single one of their penitents who was certain to have remembered all the thoughts, the desires, all the criminal aspirations of the poor sinful heart? They are well aware that to count the thoughts of the mind for days and weeks gone by, and to narrate those thoughts accurately at a subsequent period, are just as easy as to weigh and count the clouds which have passed over the sun in a three days' storm, a month after that storm is over. It is simply impossible—absurd! This has never been, this will never be done. But there is no possible peace so long as the penitent is not sure that he has remembered, counted, and confessed every past sinful thought, word and deed. It is, then, impossible, yes! it is morally and physically impossible for a soul to find peace through auricular confession. If the law which says to every sinner: "You are bound, under pain of eternal damnation, to remember all your bad thoughts and confess them to the best of your memory," were not so evidently a satanic invention, it ought to be put among the most infamous ideas which have ever come out of the brain of fallen men. For who can remember and count the thoughts of a week, of a day, nay, of an hour of this sinful life?

Where is the traveler who has crossed the swampy forests of America, in the three months of warm weather, who could tell the number of mosquitoes which have bitten him and drawn the blood from the veins? What should that traveler think of the man who, seriously, would tell him "You must prepare yourself to die, if you do not tell me, to the best of your memory, how many times you have been bitten by the mosquitoes the last three summer months, when you crossed the swampy lands along the shores of the Mississippi and Missouri rivers?" Would he not suspect that his merciless inquirer had escaped from a lunatic asylum?

But it would be much more easy for that traveler to say how many times he has suffered from the bitings of the mosquitoes, than for the poor sinner to count the bad thoughts which have passed through his sinful heart, through any period of his life.

Though the penitent is told that he must confess his thoughts only according to his best recollection,—he will never, never know if he has done his best efforts to remember everything: he will constantly fear lest he has not done his best to count and confess them correctly.

Every honest priest, if he speak the truth, will, at once, admit that his most intelligent and pious penitents, particularly among women, are constantly tortured by the fear of having omitted to confess some sinful deeds or thoughts. Many of them, after having already made several general confessions, are constantly urged by the pricking of their conscience, to begin afresh, in the fear that their first confessions had some serious defects. Those past confessions, instead of being a source of spiritual joy and peace, are, on the contrary, like so many Damocle's swords, day and night suspended over their heads, filling their souls with the terrors of an eternal death. Sometimes, the terror-stricken consciences of those honest and pious women tell them that they were not sufficiently contrite; at another time, they reproach them for not having spoken sufficiently plain, on some things fitter to make them blush.

On many occasions, too, it has happened that sins which one confessor had declared to be venial, and which had long ceased to be confessed, another more scrupulous than the first, would declare to be damnable. Every confessor, thus knows well that he proffers what is flagrantly false, every time he dismisses his penitents after confession, with the salutation: "Go in peace, thy sins are forgiven thee."

But it is a mistake to say that the soul does not find peace in auricular confession; in many cases, peace is found. And if the reader desires to learn something of that peace, let him go to the graveyard, open the tombs, and peep into the sepulchres. What awful silence! What profound quiet! What terrible and frightful peace! You hear not even the motion of the worms that creep in, and the worms that creep out, as they feast upon the dead carcass. Such is the peace of the confessional! The soul, the intelligence, the honor, the self-respect, the conscience, are, there, sacrificed. There, they must die! Yes, the confessional is the very tomb of human conscience, a sepulchre of human honesty, dignity, and liberty; the graveyard of the human soul! By its means, man, whom God hath made in his own image, is converted into the likeness of the beast that perishes; women, created by God to be the glory and helpmate of man, is transformed into the vile and trembling slave of the priest. In the confessional, man and woman attain to the highest degree of Popish perfection; they become as dry sticks, as dead branches, as silent corpses in the hands of their confessors. Their spirits are destroyed, their consciences are stiff, their souls are ruined.

This is the supreme and perfect result achieved, in its highest victories, by the Church of Rome.

There is, verily, peace to be found in auricular confession— yes, but it is the peace of the grave!

CHAPTER IX

THE DOGMA OF AURICULAR CONFESSION
A SACRILEGIOUS IMPOSTURE

BOTH Roman Catholics and Protestants have fallen into very strange errors in reference to the words of Christ: "Whosesoever sins ye remit, they are remitted unto them; and whosesoever sins ye retain, they are retained." (St. John xx. 23.)

The first have seen in this text the inalienable attributes of God of forgiving and retaining sins transferred to sinful men; the second have most unwisely granted their position, even while attempting to refute their errors.

A little more attention to the translation of the 3rd and 6th verses of chapter xiii. of Leviticus by the Septuagint would have prevented the former from falling into their sacrilegious errors, and would have saved the latter from wasting so much time in refuting errors which refute themselves.

Many believe that the Septuagint Bible was the Bible that was generally read and used by Jesus Christ and the Hebrew people in our Saviour's days. Its language was possibly the one spoken at times by Christ and understood by His hearers. When addressing His apostles and disciples on their duties towards the spiritual lepers to whom they were to preach the ways of salvation, Christ constantly followed the very expression of the Septuagint. It was the foundation of his doctrine and the testimonial of his divine mission to which he constantly appealed: the book which was the greatest treasure of the nation.

From the beginning to the end of the Old and the New Testaments, the bodily leprosy, with which the Jewish priest had to deal, is presented as the figure of the spiritual leprosy, sin, the penalty of which our Saviour had taken upon himself, that we might be saved by his death. That spiritual leprosy was the very thing for the cleansing of which he had come to this world —for which he lived, suffered, and died. Yes, the bodily leprosy with which the priests of the Jews had to deal, was the figure of the sins which Christ was to take away by shedding His blood, and with which His disciples were to deal till the end of the world.

When speaking of the duties of the Hebrew priests towards the leper, our modern translations say: (Lev. xiii. v. 6,) "They will pronounce him clean," or (v. 3) "They will pronounce him unclean."

But this action of the priests was expressed in a very different way by the Septuagint Bible, used by Christ and the people of His time. Instead of saying, "The priest shall pronounce the leper clean," as we read in our Bible, the Septuagint version says, "The priest shall clean (katharei), or shall unclean (mianei) the leper."

No one had ever been so foolish, among the Jews, as to believe that because their Bible said clean (katharei), their priests had the miraculous and supernatural power of taking away and curing the leprosy: and we nowhere see that the Jewish priests ever had the audacity to try to persuade the people that they had ever received any supernatural and divine power to "cleanse" the leprosy, because their God, through the Bible, had said of them: "They will cleanse the leper." Both priest and people were sufficiently intelligent and honest to understand and acknowledge that, by that expression, it was only meant that the priest had the legal right to see if the leprosy was gone or not, they had only to look at certain marks indicated by God Himself, through Moses, to know whether or not God had cured the leper before he presented himself to his priest. The leper, cured by the mercy and power of God alone, before presenting himself to the priest was only declared to be clean by that priest. Thus the priest was said, by the Bible, to "clean" the leper, or the leprosy;—and in the opposite case to "unclean." (Septuagint, Leviticus xiii. v. 3, 6.)

Now, let us put what God has said, through Moses, to the priests of the old law, in reference to the bodily leprosy, face to face with what God has said, through His Son Jesus, to His apostles and His whole church, in reference to the spiritual leprosy from which Christ has delivered us on the cross.

Septuagint Bible, Levit. xiii.
"And the Priest shall look on the plague, in the skin of the flesh, and when the hair in the plague is turned white, and the plague in sight be deeper than the skin of his flesh, it is a plague of leprosy; and the priest shall look on him and UNCLEAN HIM (*mianei*).
"And the Priest shall look on him again the seventh day, and if the plague is somewhat dark and does not spread on the skin, the Priest shall CLEAN HIM (*katharei*): and he shall wash his clothes and BE CLEAN" (*katharos*).

New Testament, John xx. 23.
"Whosoever sins ye remit, they are remitted unto them; and whosoever sins ye retain they are retained."

The analogy of the diseases with which the Hebrew priests and the disciples of Christ had to deal, is striking: so the analogy of the expressions prescribing their respective duties is also striking.

When God said to the priests of the Old Law, "You shall clean the leper," and he shall be "cleaned," or "you shall unclean the leper," and he shall be "uncleaned," He only gave the legal power to see if there were any signs or indications by which they could say that God had cured the leper before he presented himself to the priest. So, when Christ said to His apostles and His whole church, "Whosoever sins ye shall forgive, shall be forgiven unto them," He only gave them the authority to say when the spiritual lepers, the sinners, had reconciled themselves to God, and received their pardon from Him and Him alone, previous to the coming to the apostles.

It is true that the priests of the Old Law had regulations from God, through Moses, which they had to follow, by which they could see and say whether or not the leprosy was gone.

If the plague spread not on the skin . . . the priest shall clean him . . . but if the priest see that the scab spread on the skin, it is leprosy: he shall "unclean" him. (Septuagint, Levit. xiii. 3, 6.)

Should any be convinced that Christ spoke the Hebrew of that day and not the Greek, and used the Old Testament in Hebrew we have only to say that the Hebrew is precisely the same as the Greek—the priest is said to clean or unclean as the case may be, precisely as in the Septuagint.

So Christ had given to His apostles and His whole church equally, infallible rules and marks to determine whether or not the spiritual leprosy was gone, that they might clean the leper and tell him,

I clean thee, or I unclean thee.	I forgive thy sins, or I retain thy sins.

I would have, indeed, many passages of the Old and New Testaments to copy, were it my intention to reproduce all the marks given by God Himself, through His prophets, or by Christ and apostles, that His ambassadors might know when they should say to the sinner that he was delivered from his iniquities. I will give only a few.

First: "And he said unto them, go ye into all the world and preach the gospel to every creature:

"He that believeth and is baptised, shall be saved: but he that believeth not shall be damned." (Mark xvi. 15. 16.)

What a strange want of memory in the Saviour of the World! He has entirely forgotten that "auricular confession," besides faith and baptism are necessary to be saved! To those who believe and are baptised, the apostles and the church are authorized by Christ to say:

"You are saved! your sins are forgiven: I clean you!"

Second: "And when ye come into a house, salute it.

"And if the house be worthy, let your peace come upon it: but if it be not worthy, let your peace return to you.

"And whosoever shall not receive you nor hear your words, when ye depart out of that house or city, shake off the dust of your feet.

"Verily, verily I say unto you, it shall be more tolerable for the land of Sodom and Gomorrah, in the day of Judgment, than for that city." (Matt. x. 12-15.)

Here, again, the Great Physician tells his disciples when the leprosy will be gone, the sins forgiven, the sinner purified. It is when the lepers, the sinners, will have welcomed his messengers, hard and received their message. Not a word about auricular confession: this great panacea of the Pope was evidently ignored by Christ.

Third: "If ye forgive men their trespasses, your heavenly father will also forgive you,—but if ye forgive not men their trespasses, neither will your Father forgive your trespasses." (Matt. vi. 14-15.)

Was it possible to give a more striking and simple rule to the apostles and the disciples that they might know when they could say to a sinner: "Thy sins are forgiven!" or, "thy sins are retained?" Here the double keys of heaven are most solemnly and publicly given to every child of Adam! As sure as there is a God in heaven and that Jesus died to save sinners, so it is sure that if one forgives the trespasses of his neighbor for the dear Saviour's sake, believing in him, his own sins have been forgiven! To the end of the world, then, let the disciples of Christ say to the sinner, "Thy sins are forgiven," not because you have confessed your sins to me, but for Christ's sake; the evidence of which is that you have forgiven those who had offended you.

Fourth: "And behold, a certain one stood up and tempted him, saying: Master, what shall I do to inherit eternal life?

"He said unto him: What is written in the law? how readest thou?

"And he, answering, said: Thou shalt love the Lord thy God with all thy heart, and with all thy soul, and with all thy strength, and with all thy mind; and thy neighbor as thyself.

"And he said unto him: Thou hast answered right; this do and thou shalt live." (Luke x. 25-28.)

What a fine opportunity for the Saviour to speak of "auricular confession" as a means given by Him to be saved! But here again Christ forgets the marvellous medicine of the Popes

Jesus, speaking absolutely like the Protestants, bids his messengers to proclaim pardon, forgiveness of sins, not to those who confess their sins to a man, but to those who love God and their neighbor. And so will His true disciples and messengers do to the end of the world!

Fifth: "And when he (the prodigal son) came to himself, he said: I will arise and go to my father, and I will say unto him, Father, I have sinned against Heaven and before thee: and I am not worthy to be called thy son: make me as one of thy hired servants.

"And he arose and came to his father. But when he was yet a great way off, his father saw him and had compassion, and ran, and he fell on his neck and kissed him.

"And the son said, Father, I have sinned against Heaven and in thy sight, and am not worthy to be called thy son.

"But the father said to his servants: Bring forth the best robe, and put it on him: put a ring on his hand and shoes on his feet, and bring hither the fatted calf. For this my son was dead, and he is alive again, he was lost and he is found." (Luke xv. 17-24.)

Apostles and disciples of Christ, wherever you will hear, on this land of sin and misery, the cry of the Prodigal Son: "I will arise and go to my Father," every time you see him, not at your feet, but at the feet of his true Father, crying, "Father, I have sinned against thee," unite your hymns of joy to the joyful songs of the angels of God; repeat into the ears of that redeemed sinner the sentence just fallen from the lips of the Lamb, whose blood cleanses us from all our sins; say to him, "Thy sins are forgiven."

Sixth: "Come unto me all ye who labor, and are heavy laden, and I will give you rest. Take my yoke upon you, and learn of me, for I am meek and lowly in heart, and ye shall find rest unto your souls; for my yoke is easy and my burden is light." (Matt. xi. 28-30.)

Though these words were pronounced more than 1800 years ago, they were pronounced this very morning: they come at every hour of day and night from the lips and the heart of Christ to every one of us sinners. It is just now that Jesus says to every sinner, "Come to me and I will give ye rest." Christ has never said and He will never say to any sinner, "Go to my priests and they will give you rest." But He has said, "Come to me, and I will give you rest."

Let the apostles and disciples of the Saviour, then, proclaim peace, pardon, and rest, not to the sinners who come to confess to them all their sins, but to those who go to Christ, and Him alone, for peace, pardon and rest. For "Come to me," from Jesus' lips, has never meant—it will never mean—"Go and confess to the priests."

Christ would never have said: "My yoke is easy and my burden light" if he had instituted auricular confession. For the world has never seen a yoke so heavy, humiliating, and degrading, as auricular confession.

Seventh: "As Moses lifted up the serpent in the wilderness, even so must the Son of Man be lifted up; that whosoever believeth in Him should not perish, but have eternal life." (John iii. 14.)

Did Almighty God require any auricular confession in the wilderness, from the sinners, when he ordered Moses to lift up the serpent? No! Neither did Christ speak of auricular confession as a condition of salvation to those who look to Him when He dies on the Cross to pay their debts. A free pardon was offered to the Israelites who looked to the uplifted serpent. A free pardon is offered by Christ crucified to all those who look to Him with faith, repentance, and love. To such sinners the ministers of Christ, to the end of the world, are authorized to say: "Your sins are forgiven"—we "clean your leprosy."

Eighth: "For God so loved the world, that He gave His only begotten Son, that whosoever believeth in Him should not perish, but have everlasting life.

"For God sent not his Son to condemn the world, but that the world, through Him, might be saved.

"He that believeth in Him is not condemned; but he that believeth not is condemned already, because he hath not believed in the name of the only begotten Son of God.

"And this is the condemnation, that light is come into the world, and men loved darkness rather than light, because their deeds were evil. For every one that doeth evil, hateth the light, neither cometh to the light, lest his deeds should be reproved.

"But he that doeth truth, cometh to the light, that his deeds may be manifest, that they are wrought in God." (John iii. 16-21.)

In the religion of Rome, it is only through auricular confession that the sinner can be reconciled to God; it is only after he has heard a most detailed confession of all the thoughts, desires, and actions of the guilty one that he can tell him: "Thy sins are forgiven." But in the religion of the Gospel, the reconciliation of the sinner with his God is absolutely and entirely the work of Christ. That marvellous forgiveness is a free gift offered not for any outward act of the sinner: nothing is required from him but faith, repentance, and love. These are marks by which the leprosy is known to be cured and the sins forgiven. To all those who have these marks, the ambassadors of Christ are authorized to say, "Your sins are forgiven," we "clean" you.

Ninth: "The publican, standing afar off, would not lift up so much as his eyes to heaven, but smote upon his breast, saying: "God! be merciful to me a sinner!

"I tell you, this man went down to his house justified." (Luke xviii. 13-14.) Yes! justified! and without auricular confession.

Ministers and disciples of Christ, when you see the repenting sinner smiting his breast and crying: "Oh, God, have mercy upon me, a sinner!" shut your ears to the deceptive words of Rome, or its ugly tail the Ritualists, who tell you to force that redeemed sinner to make to you a special confession of all his sins to get his pardon. But go to him and deliver the message of love, peace, and mercy, which you received from Christ: "Thy sins are forgiven! I 'clean' thee!"

Tenth: "And one of the malefactors which were hanged, railed on him, saying: If thou be Christ save thyself and us.

"But the other, answering, rebuked him, saying: Dost thou not fear God, seeing thou art in the same condemnation?

"And we indeed justily, for we receive the due reward of our deeds: but this man hath done nothing amiss.

"And he said unto Jesus: Remember me when thou comest into thy Kingdom. And Jesus said unto him: Verily I say unto thee, to-day, shalt thou be with me in Paradise. (Luke xxiii. 39-43.)

Yes, in the Paradise or Kingdom of Christ, without auricular confession! From Calvary, when His hands are nailed to the cross, and His blood is poured out, Christ protests against the great imposture of auricular confession. Jesus will be, to the end of the world, what He was, there, on the cross: the sinner's friend; always ready to hear and pardon those who invoke His name and trust in Him.

Disciples of the gospel, wherever you hear the cry of the repenting sinner to the crucified Saviour: "Remember me when thou comest to thy Kingdom," go and give the assurance to that penitent and redeemed child of Adam, that "his sins are forgiven:"—"clean the leper."

Eleventh: "Let the wicked forsake his ways, and the unrighteous man his thoughts: and let him return to the Lord, and he will have mercy upon him; and to our God, for he will abundantly pardon." (Isa lv. 7, 8.)

"Wash you and make you clean, put away the evils of your doings from before mine eyes: cease to do evil, learn to do well; seek judgment, relieve the oppressed; judge the fatherless, and plead for the widow.

"Come now, and let us reason together, saith the Lord: though your sins be as scarlet, they will be as white as snow; though they be red like crimson, they shall be as wool." (Isa. i, 16-18.)

Here are the landmarks of the mercy of God, put by his own Almighty hands! Who will dare to remove them in order to put others in their place? Has ever Christ touched these landmarks? Has He ever intimated that anything but faith, repentance, and love, with their blessed fruits, were required from the sinner to secure His pardon? No—never.

Have the prophets of the Old Testament or the apostles of the New, ever said a word about "auricular confession," as a condition for pardon? No—never.

What does David say? "I confess my sins unto thee, and mine iniquity have I not hid. I said, I will confess my transgression unto the Lord, and thou forgavest the iniquity of my sin." (Psalm xxxii. 5.)

What does the apostle John say? "If we say that we have fellowship with him, and walk in darkness, we lie, and do not the truth.

"But if we walk in the light, as he is in the light, we have fellowship with one another, and the blood of Jesus Christ, his son, cleanseth us from sin;

"If we say we have no sin, we deceive ourselves, and the truth is not in us.

"If we confess our sins, he is faithful and just to forgive our sins, and to cleanse us from all unrighteousness." (1 John i. 6-9.) .

This is the language of the prophets and apostles. This is the language of the Old and the New Testament. It is to God and Him alone that the sinner is requested to confess his sins. It is from God and Him alone that he can expect his pardon.

The apostle Paul writes fifteen epistles, in which he speaks of all the duties imposed upon human conscience by the laws of God and the prescriptions of the Gospel of Christ. A thousand times he speaks to sinners, and tells them how they may be reconciled to God. But does he say a word about auricular confession? No—not one!

The apostles Peter, John, Jude, address six letters to the different churches, in which they state, with the greatest detail, what the different classes of sinners have to do to be saved. But again, not a single word comes from them about auricular confession.

St. James says: "Confess your faults one to another." But this is so evidently the repetition of what the Saviour had said about the way of reconciliation between those who had offended one another, and it is so far from the dogma of a secret confession to the priest that the most zealous supporters of auricular confession have not dared to mention that text in favor of their modern invention.

But if we look in vain in the Old and New Testaments for a word in favor of auricular confession as a dogma, will it be possible to find that dogma in the records of the first thousand years of Christianity? No! for the more one studies the records of the Christian Church during those first ten centuries, the more he will be convinced that auricular confession is a miserable imposture of the darkest days of the world and the church.

And so it is with the lives of several of the early fathers of the church. Not a word is said of their confessing their sins to anyone, though a thousand things are said of them which are of a far less interesting character.

So it is with the life of St. Mary, the Egyptian. The minute history of her life, her public scandals, her conversion, long prayers and fastings in solitude, the detailed history of her last days and of her death, all these we have; but not a single word is said of her confessing to anyone. It is evident that she lived and died without ever having thought of going to confess.

The deacon Pontius wrote also the life of St. Cyprian, who lived in the third century; but he does not say a word of his ever having gone to confession, or having heard the confession of anyone. More than that, we learn from this reliable historian that Cyprian was excommunicated by the Pope of Rome, called Stephen, and that he died without having ever asked from anyone absolution from that excommunication; a thing which has not seemingly prevented him from going to Heaven, since the infallible Popes of Rome, who succeded Stephen, have assured us that he is a saint.

Gregory of Nyssa has given us the life of St. Gregory, of Neo-Cæsarea, of the third century, and of St. Basil, of the fourth century. But neither speak of their having gone to confess, or having heard the secret and auricular confession of anyone. It is thus evident that those two great and good men, with all the Christians of their times, lived and died without ever knowing anything about the dogma of auricular confession.

We have the interesting life of St. Ambrose, of the fourth century, by Paulinus; and from that book it is evident, as two and two make four, that St. Ambrose never went to confess.

The history of St. Martin, of Tours, of the fourth century, by Severus Sulpicius, of the fifth century, is another monument left by antiquity to prove that there was no dogma of auricular confession in those days; for St. Martin has evidently lived and died without ever going to confess.

Pallas and Theoderet have left us the history of the life, sufferings, and death of St. Chrysostom, Bishop of Constantinople, who died ac the beginning of the fifth century, and both are absolutely mute about that dogma. No fact is more evident, by what they say, than that holy and eloquent bishop lived and died also without ever thinking of going to confess.

No man has ever more perfectly entered into the details of a Christian life, when writing on that subject, than the learned and eloquent St. Jerome, of the fifth century. Many of his admirable letters are written to the priests of his day, and to several Christian ladies and virgins, who had requested him to give them some good advice about the best way to lead a Christian life. His letters, which form five volumes, are most interesting monuments of the manners, habits, views, morality, practical and dogmatical faith of the first centuries of the church; they are a most unanswerable evidence that auricular confession, as a dogma, had then no existence, and is quite a modern invention. Would it be possible that Jerome had forgotten to give some advices or rules about auricular confession, to the priests of his time who asked his council about the best way to fulfill their ministerial duties, if it had been one of their duties to hear the confessions of the people? But we challenge the most devoted modern priest of Rome to find a single line in all the letters of St. Jerome in favor of auricular confession. In his admirable letter to the Priest Nepotianus, on the life of priests, vol. II., p. 203, when speaking of the relations of priests with women, he says: "Solus cum sola, secreto et absque arbitrio, vel teste, non sedeas. Si familarius est aliquid loquendum, habet nutricem majorem domus, virginem, viduam, vel maritatam; non est tam inhumana ut nullum præter te habeat cui se audeat credere."

"Never sit in secret, alone, in a retired place, with a female who is alone with you. If she has any particular thing to tell you, let her take the female attendant of the house, a young girl, a widow, or a married woman. She cannot be so ignorant of the rules of human life as to expect to have you as the only one to whom she can trust those things."

It would be easy to cite a great number of other remarkable passages where Jerome showed himself the most determined and implacable opponent of those secret tête-á-tête between a priest and a female, which, under the plausible pretext of mutual advice and spiritual consolation, are generally nothing but bottomless pits of infamy and perdition for both. But this is enough.

We have also the admirable life of St. Paulina, written by St. Jerome. And, though in it, he gives us every imaginable detail of her life when young, married, and widow; though he tells us even how her bed was composed of the simplest and rudest materials; he has not a word about her ever having gone to confess. Jerome speaks of the acquaintances of St. Paulina, and gives their names; he enters into the minute details of her long voyages, her charities, her foundations of monasteries for men and women, her temptations, human frailties, heroic virtues, her macerations, and her holy death; but he has not a word to say about the frequent or oracular confessions of St. Paulina; not a word about her wisdom in the choice of a prudent and holy (?) confessor.

He tells us that after her death, her body was carried to her grave on the shoulders of bishops and priests, as a token of their profound respect for the saint. But he never says that any of those priests sat there, in a dark corner with her, and forced her to reveal to their ears the secret history of all the thoughts, desires, and human frailties of her long and eventful life. Jerome is an unimpeachable witness that his saintly and noble friend, St. Paulina, lived and died without having ever thought of going to confess.

Possidius has left us the interesting life of St. Augustine, of the fifth century; and, again, it is in vain that we look for the place and time when that celebrated Bishop of Hippo went to confess, or heard the secret confessions of his people.

More than that, St. Augustine has written a most admirable book called: "Confessions," in which he gives us the history of his life. With that marvellous book in hand we follow him step by step, wherever he goes; we attend with him those celebrated schools, where his faith and morality were so sadly wrecked; he takes us with him into the garden where, wavering between heaven and hell, bathed in tears, he goes under the fig-tree and cries "Oh Lord! how long will I remain in my iniquities!" Our soul thrills with emotions, with his soul, when we hear with him, the sweet and mysterious voice: "Tolle! lege!" take and read. We run with him to the place where he has left his gospel book; with a trembling hand, we open it and we read: "Let us walk honestly as in the day . . . put ye on the Lord Jesus Christ . . ." (Rom. xiii. 13, 14.)

That incomparable book of St. Augustine makes us weep and shout with joy with him; it initiates us into all his most secret actions, to all his sorrows, anxieties, and joys; it reveals and unveils his whole life. It tells us where he goes, with whom he sins, and with whom he praises God; it makes us pray, sing, and bless the Lord with him. Is it possible that Augustine could have been to confess without telling us when, where, and to whom he made that auricular confession? Could he have received the absolution and pardon of his sins from his confessor, without making us partakers of his joys, and requesting us to bless that confessor with him?

But it is in vain that you look in that book for a single word about auricular confession. That book is an unimpeachable witness that both Augustine and his saintly mother, Monica, whom it mentions so often, lived and died without ever having been to confess. That book may be called the most crushing evidence to prove that "the dogma of auricular confession" is a modern imposture.

From the beginning to the end of that book, we see that Augustine believed and said that God alone could forgive the sins of men, and that it was to Him alone that men had to confess in order to be pardoned. If he writes his confession, it is only that the world might know how God had been merciful to him, and that they might help him to praise and bless his merciful heavenly father. In the tenth book of his Confessions, Chapter III, Augustine protests against the idea that men could do anything to cure the spiritual leper, or forgive the sins of their fellowmen; here is his eloquent protest: "Quid mihi ergo est cum hominibus ut audiant confessiones, meas, quasi ipsi sanaturi sint languores meas? Curiosum genus ad cognescendam vitam alienam; desidiosum ad corrigendam."

"What have I to do with men that they should hear my confessions, as if they were able to heal my infirmities? The human race is very curious to know another person's life, but very lazy to correct it."

Before Augustine had built up that sublime and imperishable monument against auricular confession, St. John Chrysostom had raised his eloquent voice against it in his homily on the 50th Psalm, where, speaking in the name of the church, he said: "We do not request you to go to confess your sins to any of your fellow-men, but only to God!

Nestorius, of the fourth century, the predecessor of John Chrysostom, had, by a public defence, which the best Roman Catholic historians have had to acknowledge, solemnly forbidden the practice of auricular confession. For, just as there has always been thieves, drunkards, and malefactors in the world, so there has always been men and women who, under the pretext of opening their minds to each other for mutual comfort and edification, were giving themselves to every kind of iniquity and lust. The celebrated Chrysostom was only giving the sanction of his authority to what his predecessor had done, when, thundering against the newly-born monster, he said to the Christians of his time, "We do not ask you to go and confess your iniquities to a sinful man for pardon—but only to God." (Homily on 50th Psalm.)

Auricular confession originated with the early heretics, especially with Marcion. Bellarmin speaks of it as something to be practiced. But let us hear what the contemporary writers have to say on the question.

"Certain women were in the habit of going to the heretic Marcion to confess their sins to him. But, as he was smitten with their beauty, and they loved him also, they abandoned themselves to sin with him."

Listen now to what St. Basil in his commentary on Ps. xxxvii, says of confession:

"I have not come before the world to make a confession with my lips. But I close my eyes, and confess my sins in the secret of my heart. Before thee, O God, I pour out my sighs, and thou alone art the witness. My groans are within my soul. There is no need of many words to confess: sorrow and regret are the best confession. Yes, the lamentations of the soul, which thou art pleased to hear, are the best confession."

Chrysostom, in his homily, De Pænitentia, vol. IV., col. 901, has the following: "You need no witnesses of your confession. Secretly acknowledge your sins, and let God alone hear you."

In his homily V., De incomprehensibili De natura, vol. I., he says: "Therefore, I beseech you, always confess your sins to God! I, in no way, ask you to confess them to me. To God alone should you expose the wounds of your soul, and from him alone expect the cure. Go to Him, then, and you shall not be cast off, but healed. For, before you utter a single word, God knows your prayer."

In his commentary on Heb. XII., hom. XXXI., vol. XII., p. 289, he further says: "Let us not be content with calling ourselves sinners. But let us examine and number our sins. And then I do not tell you to go and confess them, according to the caprice of some; but I will say to you, with the prophet: 'Confess your sins before God, acknowledge your iniquities at the feet of your Judge; pray in your heart and your mind, if not with your tongue, and you shall be pardoned.'"

In his homily on Ps. 1., vol. V., p. 589, the same Chrysostom says: "Confess your sins every day in prayer. Why should you hesitate to do so? I do not tell you to go and confess to a man, sinner as you are, and who might despise you if he knew your faults. But confess them to God, who can forgive them to you."

In his admirable homily IV., De Lazaro, vol. I., p. 757, he exclaims: "Why, tell me, should you be ashamed to confess your sins? Do we compel you to reveal them to a man, who might, one day, throw them into your face? Are you commanded to confess them to one of your equals, who could publish them and ruin you? What we ask of you is simply to show the sores of your soul to your Lord and Master, who is also your friend, your guardian, and physician."

In a small work of Chrysostom's, entitled, "Catethesis ad illuminandos," vol. II., p. 210, we read these remarkable words: "What we should most admire is not that God forgives our sins, but that he does not disclose them to anyone, nor wishes us to do so. What he demands of us is to confess our transgressions to him alone to obtain pardon."

St. Augustine, in his beautiful homily on the 31st Ps., says: "I shall confess my sins to God, and He will pardon all my iniquities. And such confession is not made with the lips, but with the heart only. I had hardly opened my mouth to confess my sins when they were pardoned, for God had already heard the voice of my heart."

In the edition of the Fathers by Migne, vol. 67, pp. 614, 615, we read: "About the year 390, the office of penitentiary was abolished in the church in consequence of a great scandal given by a woman who publicly accused herself of having committed a crime against chastity with a deacon."

I know that the advocates of auricular confession present to their silly dupes several passages of the Holy Fathers, where it is said that sinners were going to that priest or that bishop to confess their sins: but this is a most dishonest way of presenting that fact—for it is evident to all those who are a little acquainted with the church history of those times, that these referred only to the public confessions for public transgressions through the office of the penitentiary.

The office of the penitentiary was this:—In every large city, a priest or minister was specially appointed to preside over the church meetings where the members who had committed public sins were obliged to confess then publicly before the assembly, in order to be reinstated in the privileges of their membership: and that minister had the charge of reading or pronouncing the sentence of pardon granted by the church to the guilty ones before they could be admitted again to communion. This was perfectly in accordance with what St. Paul had done with regard to the incestuous one of Corinth; that scandalous sinner who had cast obloquy on the Christian name, but who, after confessing and weeping over his sins before the church, obtained his pardon—not from a priest in whose ears he had whispered all the details of his incestuous intercourse, but from the whole church assembled. St. Paul gladly approves the Church of Corinth in thus absolving, and receiving again in their midst, a wandering but repenting brother.

When the Holy Fathers of the first centuries speak of "confession" they invariably understand "public confessions" and not auricular confession.

There is as much difference between such public confessions and auricular confessions, as there is between heaven and hell, between God and his great enemy, Satan.

Public confession, then, dates from the time of the apostles, and is still practiced in Protestant churches of our day. But auricular confession was unknown by the first disciples of Christ; as it is rejected to-day, with horror, by all the true followers of the Son of God.

Erasmus, one of the most learned Roman Catholics who opposed the Reformation in the sixteenth century, so admirably begun by Luther and Calvin, fearlessly and honestly makes the following declaration in his treatise, De Pænitentia, Dis. 5: "This institution of penance (auricular confession) began rather of some tradition of the Old or New Testament. But our divines, not advisedly considering what the old doctors do say, are deceived, that which they say of general and open confession, they wrest, by and by, to this secret and privy kind of confession."

It is a public fact, which no learned Roman Catholic has ever denied, that auricular confession became a dogma and obligatory practice of the church only at the Council of Lateran in the year 1215, under the Pope Innocent III. Not a single trace of auricular confession, as a dogma, can be found before that year.

Thus, it has taken more than twelve hundred years of efforts for Satan to bring out this masterpiece of his inventions to conquer the world and destroy the souls of men.

Little by little, that imposture had crept into the world, just as the shadows of a stormy night creep without anyone being able to note the moment when the first rays of light gave way before the dark clouds. We know very well when the sun was shining, we know when it was very dark all over the world; but no one can tell positively when the first rays of light faded away. So saith the Lord:

"The kingdom of Heaven is likened unto a man which sowed good seed in his field.

"But while men slept, his enemy came and sowed tares among the wheat and went his way.

"But when the blade was sprung up, and brought forth fruit, there appeared the tares also.

"So the servants of the householder came and said unto him: Sir, didst not thou sow good seed in thy field? From whence then hath it tares?

"He said unto them: An enemy hath done this." (Matt. xiii. 24-28.)

Yes, the Good Master tells us that the enemy sowed those tares in his field during the night—when men were sleeping.

But he does not tell us precisely the hour of the night when the enemy cast the tares among the wheat.

However, if anyone likes to know how fearfully dark was the night which covered the "Kingdom," and how cruel, implacable, and savage was the enemy who sowed the tares, let him read the testimony of the most devoted and learned cardinals whom Rome has ever had, Baronius, Annals, Anno 900:

"It is evident that one can scarcely believe what unworthy, base, execrable, and abominable things the holy Apostolic See, which is the pivot upon which the whole Catholic Church revolves, was forced to endure, when princes of the age, though Christians, arrogated to themselves the election of the Roman Pontiffs. Alas, the shame! alas, the grief! What monsters, horrible to behold, were then intruded on the Holy See! What evils ensued! What tragedies they perpetrated! With what pollutions was this See, though itself without spot, then stained! With what corruptions infected! With what filthiness defiled! And by these things blackened with perpetual infamy! (Baronius, Annals, Anno, 900.)

"Est planè, ut vix aliquis credat, immo, nec vix quidem sit crediturus, nisi suis inspiciat ipse oculis, manibusque contractat, quam indigna, quamque turpia atque deformia, execranda insuper et abominanda sit coacta pati sacrosancta apostolica sedes, in cujus cardine universa Ecclesia catholica vertitur, cum principes sæculi hujus, quantumlibet christiani, hac tamen ex parte dicendi tyrrani sævissimi, arrogaverunt sibi, tirannice, electionem Romanorum pontificum. Quot tunc ab eis, proh pudor!! pro dolor! in eamdem sedem, angelis reverandam, visu horrenda intrusa sunt monstra? Quot ex eis oborta sunt mala, consummatæ tragediæ! Quibus tunc ipsam sine maculâ et sine rugâ contigit aspergi sordibus, purtoribus infici, in quinati spurcitiis, ex hisque perpetuâ infamiâ denigrari!"

CHAPTER X

THE Priests of Rome resort to various means in order to deceive the people on the immorality resulting from auricular confession. One of their favorite stratagems is to quote some disconnected passages from theologians, recommending caution on the part of the priest, in questioning his penitents on delicate subjects, should he see or apprehend any danger for the latter of being shocked by his questions. True, there are such prudent theologians, who seem to realize more than others the real danger of the priest in confession. But those wise counselors resemble very much a father who would allow his child to put his fingers in the fire, while advising him to be cautious lest he should burn those fingers. There is just as much wisdom in the one case as there would be in the other. What would you say of a brutal parent casting a young, weak and inexperienced boy among wild beasts, with the foolish and cruel expectation that his prudence might save him from injury?

Such theologians may be perfectly honest in giving such advice, although it is anything but wise or reasonable. But those are far from being honest or true who contend that the Church of Rome, in commanding everyone to confess all his sins to the priests, has made an exception in favor of sins against chastity. This is only so much dust thrown in the eyes of Protestants and ignorant people, to prevent them from seeing through the frightful mysteries of confession.

When the Council of Lateran decided that every adult, of either sex, should confess all their sins to a priest, at least once a year, there was no exceptions made for any special class of sins, not even for those committed against modesty or purity. And when the Council of Trent ratified or renewed the previous decision, no exception was made, either, of the sins in question. They were expected and ordered to be confessed, as all other sins.

The law of both Councils is still unrepealed and binding for all sins, without any exception. It is imperative, absolute; and every good Catholic, man or woman, must submit to it by confessing all his or her sins, at least once a year.

I have in my hand Butler's Catechism, approved by several bishops of Quebec. On page 62, it reads, "that all penitents should examine themselves on the capital sins, and confess them all, without exception, under penalty of eternal damnation."

The celebrated controversial catechism of Rd. Stephen Keenan, approved by all the bishops of Ireland, positively says (page 186) : "The penitent must confess all his sins."

Therefore, the young and timid girl, the chaste and modest woman, must think of shameful deeds and fill their minds with impure ideas, in order to confess to an unmarried man whatever they may be guilty of, however repugnant may be to them such confession, or dangerous to the priest who is bound to hear and even demand it. No one is exempt from the loathsome, and often polluting task. Both priest and penitent are required and compelled to go through the fiery ordeal of contamination and shame. They are bound, on every particular, the one to ask, and the other to answer, under penalty of eternal damnation.

Such is the rigorous, inflexible law of the Church of Rome with regard to confession. It is taught not only in works of theology or from the pulpit, but in prayer-books and various other religious publications. It is so deeply impressed in the minds of Romanists as to have become a part of their religion. Such is the law which the priest himself has to obey, and which puts his penitents at his own discretion.

But there are husbands with a jealous disposition, who would little fancy the idea of bachelors confessing their wives, if they knew exactly what questions they have to answer in confession. There are fathers and mothers who don't like much to see their daughters alone with a man, behind a curtain, and who would certainly tremble for their honor and virtue if they knew all the abominable mysteries of confession. It is necessary, therefore, to keep these people, as much as possible, in ignorance, and prevent light from reaching that empire of darkness, the confessional. In that view, confessors are advised to be cautious "on those matters"; to "broach these questions in a sort of covert way, and with the greatest reserve." For it is very desirable "not to shock modesty, neither frighten the penitent nor grieve her. Sins, however, must be confessed."

Such is the prudent advice given to the confessor on certain occasions. In the hands or under the command of Liguori, Father Gury, Scavani, or other casuists, the priest is a sort of general, sent during the night, to storm a citadel or a strong position, having for order to operate cautiously, and before daylight. His mission is one of darkness and violence, and cruelty; above all, it is a mission of supreme cunning, for when the Pope commands, the priest, as his loyal soldier, must be ready to obey; but always with a mask or blind before him, to conceal his object. However, many a time, after the place has been captured by dint of strategy and secrecy, the poor soldier is left, badly wounded and completely disabled, on the battle-field. He has paid dearly for his victory; but the conquered citadel has also received an injury from which it may never recover. The crafty priest has gained his point: he has succeeded in persuading his lady penitent that there was no impropriety, that it was even necessary for them to have a parley on things that made her blush a few moments before. She is soon so well convinced, that she would swear that there is nothing wrong in confession. Truly this is a fulfillment of the words: "Abyssus abyssum invocat," an abyss calls for another abyss.

Have the Romish theologians—Gury, Scavani, Liguori, etc.—ever been honest enough, in their works on confession, to say that the Most Holy God could never command or require woman to degrade and pollute herself and the priest in pouring into the ear of a frail and sinful mortal, words unfit even for an angel? No; they were very careful not to say so; for, from that very moment, their shameless lies would have been exposed; the stupendous, but weak structure of auricular confession, would fall to the ground, with sad havoc and ruin to its unholders. Men and women would open their eyes, and see its weakness and fallacy. "If God," they might say, "can forgive our most grievous sins against modesty, without confessing them, He can and will certainly do the same with those of less gravity; therefore there is no necessity or occasion for us to confess to a priest."

But those shrewd casuists knew too well that, by such frank declaration, they would soon lose their hold on Catholic populations, especially on women, by whom, through confession, they rule the world. They much prefer to keep their grip on benighted minds, frightened consciences, and trembling souls. No wonder, then, that they fully endorse and confirm the decisions of the councils of Lateran and Trent, ordering "that all sins must be confessed such as God knows them." No wonder that they try their best or worst to overcome the natural repugnance of women for making such confessions, and to conceal the terrible dangers for the priests in hearing the same.

However, God, in his infinite mercy, and for the sake of truth, has compelled the Church of Rome to acknowledge the moral dangers and corrupting tendencies of auricular confession. In His eternal wisdom, He knew that Roman Catholics would close their ears to whatever might be said by the disciples of gospel truth, of the demoralising influence of that institution; that they would even reply with insult and fallacy to the words of truth kindly addressed to them, just as the Jews of old returned hatred and insult to the good Saviour who was bringing them the glad tidings of a free salvation. He knew that Romish devotees, led astray by their priests, would call the apostles of truth, liars, seducers, possessed of the devil, as Christ was constantly called a demoniac, an impostor, and finally put to death by His false accusers.

That great God, as compassionate now as He was then for the

poor benighted and deluded souls, has wrought a real miracle to open the eyes of the Roman Catholics, and compel them, as it were, to believe us, when we say, on His authority, that auricular confession was invented by Satan to ruin both the priest and his female penitents, for time and eternity. For, what we would never have dared to say of ourself to the Roman Catholics with regard to what frequently happens between their priests and their wives and daughters, either during or after confession, God has constrained the Church of Rome to acknowledge herself, in revealing things that would have seemed incredible, had they come simply from our mouth or our pen. In this, as in other instances, that apostate Church has unwittingly been the mouthpiece of God for the accomplishment of His great and merciful ends.

Listen to the questions that the Church of Rome, through her theologians, puts to every priest after he has heard the confession of your wives or daughters:

1. "Nonne inter audiendas confessiones quasdam proposui questiones circa sextum decalogi preæceptum cum intentione libidinosa? (Miroir du Clergé, p. 582.)

"While hearing confessions, have I not asked questions on sins against the sixth (seventh in the Decalogue) commandment, with the intention of satisfying my evil passions?"

Such is the man, O mothers and daughters, to whom you dare to unbosom the most secret, as well as the most shameful actions. You kneel down at his feet and whisper in his ear your most intimate thoughts and desires, and your most polluting deeds; because your church, by dint of cunning and sophistry, has succeeded in persuading you that there was no impropriety or danger in doing so; that the man whom you choose for your spiritual guide and confident, could never be tempted or tainted by such foul recitals. But that same Church, through some mysterious providence, is made to acknowledge, in her own books, her own lies. In spite of herself, she admits that there is real danger in confession, both for the woman and for the priest; that willingly or otherwise, and sometimes both unawares, they lay for each other dangerous snares. The Church of Rome, as if she had an evil conscience for allowing her priest to hold such close and secret converse with a woman, on such delicate subjects, keeps, as it were, a watchful eye on him, while the poor misguided woman is pouring in his ear the filthy burden of her soul; and as soon as she is off, questions the priest as to the purity of his motives, the honesty of his intentions in putting the requisite questions. "Have you not," she asks him immediately, "under the pretence of helping that woman in her confession, put to her certain questions simply in order to gratify your lust, and with the object of satisfying your evil propensities?"

2. "Nonne munus audiendi confessiones suscepi, aut peregi ex prava incontinentiœ appettentia?" (Idem, p. 582.) "Have I not repaired to the confessional and heard confessions with the intention of gratifying my evil passions?" (Miroir du Clerge, p. 582.)

O ye women! who tremble like slaves at the feet of the priests, you admire the patience and charity of those good (?) priests, who are willing to spend so many long and tedious hours in hearing the confession of your secret sins; and you hardly know how to express your gratitude for so much kindness and charity. But, hush, listen to the voice of God speaking to the conscience of the priest, through the Church of Rome!

"Have you not," she asks him, "heard the confession of women simply to foster or gratify the grovelling passions of your fallen nature and corrupt heart?"

Please notice, it is not I, or the enemies of your religion, who put to your priests the above questions; it is God Himself, who, in His pity and compassion for you, compels your own Church to ask such questions; that your eyes may be opened, and that you may be rescued from all the dangerous obscenities and the humiliating and degrading slavery of auricular confession. It is God's will to deliver you from such bondage and degradation. In His tender mercies He has provided means to drag you out of that cesspool, called confession; to break the chains which bind you to the feet of a miserable and blasphemous sinner called confessor, who, under the pretence of being able to pardon your sins, usurps the place of your Saviour and your God! For while you are whispering your sins in his ear, God says to him through his Church, in tones loud enough to be heard: "In hearing the confession of these women, are you not actuated by lust, spurred by evil passions?"

Is this not sufficient to warn you of the danger of auricular confession? Can you now, with any sense of safety or propriety, come to that priest, for whom your very confession may be a snare, a cause of fall or fearful temptation? Can you, with a particle of honor or modesty, willingly expose yourself to the impure desires of your confessors? Can you, with any sort of womanly dignity, consent to entrust that man with your inmost thoughts and desires, your most humiliating and secret actions, when you know from your own Church's lips, that that man may not have any higher object in listening to your confession than a lustful curiosity, or a sinful desire of exciting his evil passions?

3. "Nonne ex audits in confessione occasionem sumpsi pœnitentes utriusque sexus ad peccandum sollicitandi?" (Idem, p. 582.)

"Have I not availed myself of what I heard in confession to induce my penitents of both sexes to commit sin?"

I would run a great risk of being treated with the utmost contempt, should I dare to put your priests such a question. You would very likely call me a scoundrel, for daring to question the honesty and purity of such holy men. You would, perhaps, go as far as to contend that it is utterly impossible for them to be guilty of such sins as are alluded to in the above question; that never such shameful deeds have been perpetrated through confession. And you would, maybe, emphatically deny that your confessor has ever said or done anything that might lead you to sin or even commit any breach of propriety or modesty. You feel perfectly safe on that score, and see no danger to apprehend.

Let me tell you, good ladies, that you are altogether too confident, and thus you are kept in the most fatal delusion. Your own Church, through the merciful and warning voice of God speaking to the conscience of your own theologians, tells you that there is a real and imminent danger, where you fancy yourself in perfect security. You may never have suspected the danger, but it is there, within the walls of the confessional; nay, more, it is lurking in your very hearts, and that of your confessor. He may hitherto have refrained from tempting you; he may, at least, have kept within the proper limits of outward morality or decency. But nothing warrants you that he may not be tempted; and nothing could shield you from his attempts on your virtue, should he give way to temptation, as cases are not wanting to prove the truth of my assertion. You are sadly mistaken in a false and dangerous security. You are, although unawares, on the very brink of a precipice, where so many have fallen through their blind confidence in their own strength, or their confessor"s prudence and sanctity. Your own Church is very anxious about your own safety; she trembles for your innocence and purity. In her fear, she cautions the priest to be watchful over his wicked passions and human frailty. How dare you pretend to be stronger and more holy than your confessor is in the mind of your own Church? Why should you so wilfully imperil your chastity or modesty? Why expose yourself to danger, when it could be so easily avoided? How can you be so rash, so devoid of common prudence and modesty as to shamelessly put yourselves in a position to tempt and be tempted, and thereby incur your temporal and eternal perdition?

4. "Nonne extra tribunal, vel, in ipso confessionis actu, aliuqia dixi aut egi cum intenticne diabolica has personas seducendi?" (Idem, idem).

"Have I not, either during or after confession, done or said certain things with a diabolical intention of seducing my female patients?"

"What arch enemy of our holy religion is so bold and impious as to put to our saintly priests such an impudent and insulting question?" may ask some of our Roman Catholic readers. It is easy to answer. This great enemy of your religion is no less than a justly offended God, admonishing and reproving your priests for exposing both you and themselves to dangerous allurements and seductions. It is His voice speaking to their consciences, and warning them of the danger and corruption of auricular confession. It says to them: Beware! for ye might be tempted, as surely you will be, to do or say something against honor and purity.

Husbands and fathers! who rightly value the honor of your wives and daughters more than all treasures, who consider it too precious a boon to be exposed to the dangers of pollution, and who would prefer to lose your life a thousand times, than to see those you love most on earth fall in the snares of the seducer, read once more and ponder what your Church asks the priest, after he has heard your wife and daughter in confession: "Have you not, either during or after confession, done or said something with a diabolical intention of seducing your female patients?"

If your priest remains deaf to these words addressed to his conscience, you cannot help giving heed to them and understanding their full significance. You cannot be easy and fear nothing from that priest in those close interviews with your wives and daughters, when his superiors and your own Church tremble for him, and question his purity and honesty. They see a great danger for both the confessor and his penitent; for they know that confession has, many a time, been the pretence of the cause of the most shameful seductions.

If there were no real danger for the chastity of women, in confessing to a man their most secret sins, do you believe that your popes and theologians would be so stupid as to acknowledge it, and put to confessors questions that would be most insulting and out of place, should there be no occasion for them?

Is it not presumption and folly, on your part, to think that there is no danger, when the Church of Rome tells you, positively, that there is danger, and uses the strongest terms in expressing her uneasiness and apprehension?

Why! your Church sees the most pressing reasons to fear for the honor of your wives and daughters, as well as for the chastity of her priests; and still you remain unconcerned, indifferent to the fearful peril to which they are exposed! Are you like the Jewish people of old, to whom it was said: "Hear ye indeed, but understand not; and see ye indeed, but perceive not?" (Isa. vi. 9).

But if you see or suspect the danger you are warned of; if the eye of your intelligence can fathom the dreadful abyss where the dearest objects of your heart are in danger of falling, then it behoves you to keep them from the paths that lead to the fearful chasm. Do not wait till it is too late, when they are too near the precipice to be rescued. You may think the danger to be far off, while it is near at hand. Profit by the sad experience of so many victims of confession who have been irretrievably lost, irrecoverably ruined for time and eternity. The voice of your conscience, of honor, of God Himself, tells you that it may soon become too late to save them from destruction, through your neglect and procrastination. While thanking God for having preserved them from temptations that have proved fatal to so many married or unmarried women, do not lose a single moment in taking the necessary means to keep them from temptation and falls.

Instead of allowing them to go and kneel at the feet of a man to obtain the remission of their sins, lead them to the dying Saviour's feet, the only place where they can secure pardon and peace everlasting. And why, after so many unfruitful attempts, should they try any longer to wash themselves in a puddle, when the pure waters of eternal life are offered them so freely through Christ Jesus, their only Saviour and Mediator?

Instead of seeking their pardon from a poor and miserable sinner, weak and tempted as they are, let them go to Christ, the only strong and perfect man, the only hope and salvation of the world.

O poor deluded Catholic women! listen no longer to the deceiving words of the Church of Rome, who has no pardon, no peace for you, but only snares; who offers you thraldom and shame in return for the confession of your sins! But listen rather to the invitations of your Saviour, who has died on the cross, that you might be saved; and who, alone, can give rest to your weary souls.

Hearken to His words, when He says to you: "Come unto Me, O ye heavily laden, crushed, as it were, under the burden of your sins, and I shall give you rest . . . I am the Physician of your souls. . . . Those who are well have no need of a physician, but those who are sick. . . . Come, then, to Me, and ye shall be healed. . . . I have not sent back nor lost any who have come to Me. . . . invoke My name. . . . believe in Me. . . . repent. . . . love God, and your neighbor as yourself, and you shall be saved. . . . For all who believe in Me and call upon My name, shall be saved. . . . When I am raised up between heaven and earth, I shall draw every one to Me. . . ."

Oh, mothers and daughters, instead of going to the priest for pardon and salvation, go to Jesus, who is so pressingly inviting you! and the more so as you have more need of divine help and grace. Even, if you are as great a sinner as Mary Magdalene, you can, like her, wash the feet of the Saviour with the flowing tears of your repentance and your love, and like her, receive the pardon of your sins.

To Jesus, then, and to Him alone, go for the confession and pardon of your sins; for there, only, you can find peace, light, and life for time and eternity!

CHAPTER XI

WE HOPE this chapter will be read with interest and benefit everywhere; it will be particularly interesting to the people of Australia, America, and France. Let every one consider with attention its solemn teachings; they will see how auricular confession is spreading, broadcast, the seeds of an unspeakable corruption on every side, all over the world. Let every one see how the enemy is successfully at work, to destroy every vestige of honesty and purity in the hearts and the minds of the fair daughters of their countries.

Though I have been in Australia only a few months, I have a collection of authentic and undeniable facts about the destruction of female virtue, through the confessional, which would fill several large volumes, and would strike the country with horror, were it possible to publish them all. But to keep myself within the limits of a short chapter, I will give only a few of the most public ones.

Not long ago, a young Irish lady, belonging to one of the most respectable families of Ireland, went to confess to a priest of Parramatta. But the questions put to her in the confessional, were of such a bestial character; the efforts made by this priest to persuade his God-fearing and honest young penitent, to consent to satisfy the infamous desires of his corrupted heart, caused the young lady to give up, immediately, the Church of Rome, and break the fetters, by which she had been too long bound to the feet of her would-be seducers. Let the reader peruse her letter, which I have copied from the Sydney (Australia) Gazette, of the 28th July, 1839, and they will see how bravely, and over her own signature, she not only accuses her confessors of having most infamously scandalized her by their questions, and tried to destroy in her the last vestige of female modesty, but she declares that many of her female friends had acknowledged in her presence, that they had been dealt with in the very same way, by their father confessors.

As that young lady was the niece of a well-known Roman Catholic Bishop, and the near relation of two priests, her public declaration made a profound sensation in the public mind, and the Roman Catholic hierarchy keenly felt the blow. The facts were too plainly and bravely given by that unimpeachable witness to be denied. The only thing to which those haughty and implacable enemies of all that is true, holy and pure, in the world, had recourse to, to defend their tottering power, and keep their mask of honesty, what they have done in all ages—"murder the honest young girl they had not been able to silence." A few days after she was found bathed in her blood, and cruelly bruised, at a short distance from Parramatta; but by the good providence of God, the would-be murderers, sent by these priests, had failed to kill their victim. She recovered from her wounds, and lived many years more to proclaim before the public, how the priests of Australia, as well as the priests of the rest of the world, make use of auricular confession to pollute the hearts, and damn the souls of their penitents.

Here is the letter of that young, honest, and brave lady:—

THE CONFESSIONAL

(To the Editors of the Sydney Gazette)

While reading over, the other day, in the Sydney Gazette, an account of the trial, which took place at the Supreme Court, Tuesday, the 9th instant, I was struck with inexpressible amazement at the evidence of Dr. Polding, Roman Catholic Bishop in this colony, and beg to enquire, through the medium of your paper, whether any difference exists between the English and the Irish Roman Catholic priests? If there does not, and if what Dr. Polding says is really the case, I must have been very unfairly dealt with indeed by most of the priests, to whom I have confessed.

I know very well a Roman Catholic priest will never say— "Pay me so much, and I will give you absolution," because that would be exposing the craft; but practice speaks louder than precept, and I can say for myself (and I know hundreds of others, who could say the same, if they dared), that I have, times without number, paid the priest, before I rose from my knees at confession, under the pretence, as I will show, of getting masses and prayers said for the release of the souls of my deceased relatives from purgatory.

I was taught to believe that masses were not valid, unless I was from under a state of sin, or in other words, in a state of grace. Consequently I must be absolved, to make the masses effectual, and all Roman Catholics know full well, that all masses must be paid for before they will be said. I have been told by a priest, a man of good education, that the more I gave, the better for my own soul, and the souls of friends detained in purgatory. I was taught to believe that the Church of Rome being infallible, and incapable of erring, its doctrine and practices were the same throughout the world; of course I was the more staggered on reading Dr. Polding's evidence. I think that he must be laboring under a great mistake, when he says, that it is strictly forbidden for a priest to receive money in any way, or even if anything should be given for charitable purposes, it is usual to give it at another time, "but not customary," or else the priests in Ireland are outrageously simonical. Perhaps Dr. Polding will inform me, why I should, for so many years, and not only I, but very many members of my poor deluded family, pay the priest for relics—such as "the wood of the cross," "holy bones," "holy wax," "holy fire," "pieces of saints' garments," from Rome and other places; "holy clay," from the saints' tombs; "the Agnus Dei," "gospels," "scapularies," "blessed candle," "blessed salt," "St. Francis' lard," &c.

But the time would fail me to repeat the abominable delusions I've paid for, and none of them could, in any way, be reckoned among the priests' traveling expenses, as the priests were resident in the place; but, perhaps, there are not some of the acts which would bring a priest into degradation with his own community, as Dr. Polding acknowledges; "there are certain acts to which, inherently and incessantly, there are degradations and detestation attached," but I humbly and heartily thank God I have not, like Dr. Polding, to wait until I have "been a Protestant," to know how such acts must affect all who come within reach of their contagion, as I do most solemnly protest, before God and man, against refuges of lies and idolatrous worship of the Popish Church, out of which it is my earnest and constant prayer, that not only my own relations, but all within her pale, may, through the riches of God's grace, "come out from her and be separate," as I have, so that after the way—which they call heresy—"that they may yet be brought to worship the God of their fathers."

But there is one thing asserted by Dr. Polding, in his evidence, that needs particular explanations, as it either casts a most blasphemous reflection on the Holy Scriptures, or Dr. Polding must, if he directs the attention of Protestants, for the rule of confession, in the Roman Catholic Church, to the Holy Scriptures, be totally ignorant of that, which the everyday student in Maynooth College is master of; and were it not that I esteem the glory of God far beyond my own personal feelings of female delicacy, I would shrink from acknowledging that which I do now publicly, and with shame, that I have carefully perused the translations of the extracts from "Dens' Theology," where alone the true practice of the Roman Catholic confessional is to be found, and publicly authorized by Dr. Murray, the Roman Catholic Archbishop of Dublin, and in the presence of my Maker, I solemnly declare, that horrible and unspeakably vile as that book is, I have had a hundred times more disgusting questions put to me in the confessional, which I was obliged to answer.

having been told by my confessor, "that being ashamed of answering him, I was in a state of mortal sin." I have been often obliged to perform severe penance, for repeating to my companions a portion of these horrible things, out of confession, and comparing the questions put to them (as far as decency would allow) with those put to myself. What then will the Protestant public think, when I again declare, and in the same solemn manner, that their experience, and especially the experience of one of them, was worse than mine, acts following questions, which I readily believe, from the specimens offered to myself one day in the confessional.

If then, Dr. Polding will only prove to me, "from simply the Holy Scriptures," any authority for what I have stated, on the part of Roman Catholic Confession, and which may be read by any one who pleases, in Dens' Theology,—I promise to return to the bosom of the Roman Catholic Church. But I must leave this subject for the present, on which I could relate what would fill a moderate sized volume, and just speak a few words about the sale of indulgences, of which Dr. Polding has only read "in Protestant books." This also astonished me, that a bishop in the Roman Catholic Church, should know nothing of these things, and I too have purchased one, which I did during the cholera of 1832. At that time I heard the priest of the parish publish from the altar, that the Pope had granted an indulgence; and, as the cholera was raging in Dublin, every one was in dread of its spreading over the whole country, and every Roman Catholic that could crawl to the chapel, in the parish where I lived, lost no time in coming. Amongst them I well remember the priest showing me an old woman, who, he said, had not been to confession for fifty years, and who was in the act of laying her money on the tray, when he pointed her out. Indulgence was to be had, as the priest had published, and I saw the old woman put her money on the tray, where I put mine—she got her seal of indulgence, and I got mine. Will Dr. Polding have the kindness to tell me what the money was for? In complying with the indulgence, it was necessary also, to say so many prayers, such as the "Jesus Psalter," &c., but those who could not were to bring their beads to their priests, who selected a proper number of prayers to be said on them. Persons were to give at their own option, what money they pleased, but nothing less than silver was taken. I have seen trays on the vestry-room table of the chapel, at that time, full of silver, bank-notes and gold, and I have also seen trays for the same purpose, in Marlborough Street Chapel, Dublin, upon the holy-water trough.

How many poor creatures have I known, who were little short of starving, beg or borrow a six-pence, to be at the chapel at that time; but it would be impossible almost for me, unless I was as insensible as the images I was taught to worship, especially my own guardian angel, St. Agnes, to whom, with the Virgin Mary, I was taught to pay more adoration than to God Himself, were I to have remained unacquainted with the depth of these, and many more wicked and abominable devices, under the garb of the most self-denying religion, having such a number of priests related to me, a bishop for my uncle, and brought up amongst priests, friars, and nuns of almost every order, from my birth, besides being a most zealous devoted Roman Catholic myself, during my ignorance of "the truth, as it is in Jesus." But I am content to leave all temporal good as I have already done, in leaving wealthy relations and former friends, only desiring from my heart, that, as I have suffered the loss of all things, I may "be more enabled to count them but dung, that I may win Christ, and be found in Him, not having my own righteousness (which I was taught to value in the Roman Catholic Church, and which is of the law), but that which is through the faith of Christ, the righteousness, which is of God, by faith." I know, sir, I have taken up too much of your paper, but, should it please God, that the truths, the solemn truths, which I have stated, be so blessed as to rouse even one of my Roman Catholic fellow-sinners to reflect, and break through that slavish bondage, in which I know too well, they are kept, and begin to think for him or herself, I am sure you will feel doubly recompensed for the space you have given this letter.

I am, sir, &c., &c.,

Agnes Catherine Byrne.

25th July, 1839.

As some people, from a mistaken sense of charity, may be tempted to believe that the priests of Rome, in Australia, have reformed, and are not so corrupted today as they were in 1839, let them read the following document, which I take from the Sydney Evening News, 19th November, 1878:—

"One of the largest assemblages that were ever seen inside the Protestant Hall in Castlereaghstreet, attended last night in response to an advertisement announcing that a lady would deliver a lecure on the subject—'Mrs. Constable wrong, and the ex-priest Chiniquy right, relative to auricular confession; proved by the lady's personal experience in Sydney.' The building was densely packed in every part, and there was no standing room. On the platform, around it, and in the galleries were large numbers of ladies. Pastor Allen then opened the proceedings by giving out the hymn, 'Rock of ages cleft for me.' Mr. W. Neill (the banker) was voted to the chair. The lady lecturer, Mrs. Margaret Ann Dillon, a middle-aged lady, neatly dressed, was then introduced to the audience. At first she appeared somewhat tremulous and confused, which she explained was mainly owing to the cruel and heartless letter she had, that night, received, announcing the death of her husband. She stated that she had not been brought up in the Roman Catholic faith, but after much consideration she had joined that Church, because she had been led to believe it was the only true Church. She had, for years after joining the Church, faithfully attended to its duties, even to auricular confession. It was not her intention to insult the Roman Catholics that she had thus publicly come forward, but to refute the allegations of Mrs. Constable, and show that the ex-priest Chiniquy's statements were true. Nothing but her duty to God would have caused her to come before them in this public manner. It was her first appearance in public; therefore, they must allow for her short-comings; but she would speak truthfully and fearlessly. Her address would have reference entirely to her own personal experience of auricular confession. After some further remarks, Mr. Neill was requested to read the following letter, sent by the lady lecturer to Archbishop Vaughan:—'No. 259 Kent Street, Sydney. 12th of April, 1878. To his Grace Archbishop Vaughan. May it please your Grace:—I have for a considerable time past been very desirous of bringing a most painful subject under your notice, and which has caused me considerable pain. Various reasons have prevented my doing so until now, and it is only when I perceive the object of my complaint apparently unpunished for his conduct, which I heard has been the case, I determined upon appealing to you, feeling sure of obtaining redress. About the year 1876, I resided in Clarence street, in this city, and while suffering from severe illness was visited by Father Sheridan, of St. Mary's, as also by Father Maher. From the former I received the last rites of the Church, as I was supposed to be on my dying-bed. Half an hour after Father Sheridan had left me, Father Maher called upon me, and insisted upon performing the service upon me, which I declined. There was a bottle containing brandy on the table, and by its side a tumbler containing a small quantity of castor oil for my use. Father Maher wished for some of the spirits, and my husband, who was in the room, requested him to help himself. He did so, using the tumbler that contained the medicine, and finding the mistake, he had emptied some more of the spirits into a clean tumbler, and drank it. He then desired my husband to leave the room. He then came to my bedside professedly to administer the rites of the Church to me, and I remonstrated with him, when he laid violent hands upon me, and made most improper overtures to me. In my struggle to resist, my night dress was much torn. He assured me that no harm would be done to me if I did comply with his terrible device (Cries of Oh! Oh!) saying what he did was under the holy orders, and would not be held as a sin by the

Church, or words to that effect. (Sensation.) I, at length, found strength to call my husband; and, on his appearing, Father Maher was forced to leave the room. I was fearful in telling my husband all that happened, as I felt sure he would use violence to Father Maher. Since the occurrence, I was apprised that he had been suspended for some other cause, and that it was useless my taking steps in the matter. But as, within the present month, I have seen him passing my door dressed in a priest's usual garb, and it being evident to me that he is still under some control, I have determined upon making the complaint he so richly deserves. I write to add that when my husband drove him off the premises, he (Father Maher) had become quite intoxicated with the spirits he had taken.—I am, with much respect, your Grace's humble servant, Margaret Ann Dillon.' Mrs. Dillon then proceeded, at great length, to relate minutely the facts of the affair stated in the letter, and how the Vicar-General (Dean Sheridan) came to her place to hush up the matter. In a long dialogue with the reverend Dean, she asserted that he maintained that Archbishop Vaughan had shed tears over her letter, and that he (the Dean) had always known her to be a good woman. In reply to a question, the Dean told her that 'once a priest always a priest;' but she rejoined, 'once in infamy, always in infamy.' Subsequently, a priest called on her, and asked her why she did not go to church. She explained that, having three children to take care of, she could not go. Once, a priest saw the Protestant Bible with some other books on her table, and he said to her, 'I see you have got some heretical books here; you must take them and burn them.' She said she would not do so; and he said, 'If you do not give me those books, I will not give you absolution.' She said she did not care, and he left the place. The lady then read from Dens' Theology, Vol. VI., page 305, as to the doctrines of the confessional. She maintained that the priest likened themselves to God in the confessional-box, but outside of it they were only men. She would not give utterance to the filthy language that she had been subject to hear and reply to by the priest in the confessional-box. Not only herself, but her daughter could bear witness to the abominations of the confessional. She had been married twice, and shortly after her first husband's death she sent her daughter to confession. The priest told her daughter that her dead father, who had been a Protestant, was a heretic, and was in hell. She urged that Catholic women ought not to send their children to be insulted and degraded by the confessional. She hoped they would keep their children away from it, for the priests put questions to them suggesting wickedness of the grossest description, and filling their minds with carnal thoughts for the first time in their lives. (Cheers.) She would strongly advise all Roman Catholic men not to allow priests to remain alone with their wives. Napoleon adopted a scheme by which he would himself frame the questions to be put to his son in the confessional. If Napoleon was so careful of his son, how much more so must those be in a humbler sphere of life. Mrs. Dillon, then, read extracts from Den's Theology and other textbooks, which she claimed to be the standard works of the Roman Catholic Church, to refute Mrs. Constable's allegations. Her experience, as well as that of many others, clearly proved that the cause of the majority of the large numbers of girls on the streets arose from the abominable questions they have to reply to in the confessional-box (Cheers.) Not only were the majority of these girls Catholics, but our hospitals and charitable institutions are filled with those whose early life had been degraded in the confessional. (Hear, hear.) In conclusion, Mrs. Dillon touched on the sacrament question, asserting that the priests take good care to drink the wine—the blood of Christ,—and the people had the lozenge,—the body of Christ. (Laughter.) Mrs. Dillon resumed her seat amid tumultuous cheering. Frequently her remarks created great sensation and rounds of applause. The Rev. Pastor Allen read a letter sent that night to the lady lecturer, containing an extract from the S. M. Herald, published four years ago, about the punishment of an Abbe for unpriestly conduct to four young ladies in the confessional. A hearty vote of thanks was passed to the lady lecturer, and a similar honor was accorded to Mr. Neill, for presiding. The benediction and the singing of the National Anthem closed the proceedings about half-past nine o'clock.

Has the world ever seen any act more disgustingly corrupt than that priest's? Who will not be struck with horror at the sight of that confessor, who struggles with his dying penitent, and tears her night dress, when she is on her sick bed, to satisfy his vile propensities?

What an awful spectacle is here presented, by the hands of Providence, before the eyes of a Christian people! A dying woman obliged to fight and struggle against her confessor, to keep her purity and honor intact! Her night-robes torn by the beastly priest of Rome!

Let the Americans who like to know more precisely what is going on between the father confessors and their female penitents in the United States, go to the beautiful town of Malone, in the State of New York. There, they will see, by the public records of the court, how Father McNully seduced his fair penitent, Miss McFarlane, who was boarding with him, and of whom he was the teacher. They will see that the enraged parents of the young lady prosecuted him and got a verdict of $2,129 for damage, which he refused to pay. He was incarcerated—broke his gaol, went to Canada, where he was welcomed by the bishops and employed among the confessors of the Irish girls of the Dominion!

Do not the echoes of the whole world still repeat the horrors of the Cracow Nunnery in Austria? In spite of the superhuman efforts of the Roman Catholic press to suppress or deny the truth, has it not been proved by the evidence that the unfortunate Nun Barbara Ubryk was found absolutely naked in a most horrible, dark, damp, and filthy dungeon, where she had been kept by the nuns because she had refused to live their life of infamy with their Father Confessor Pankiewiez. And has not that miserable priest corroborated all that was brought to his charge, by putting an end himself, like Judas, to his own infamous life?

I have met, in Montreal, a nephew of the Nun Barbara Ubryk, who was in Cracow when his aunt was found in her horrible dungeon. He not only corroborated all what the press had said about the tortures of his near relation and their cause, but he publicly gave up the Church of Rome, whose confessional he knew personally are schools of perdition.

I visited Chicago for the first time in 1851, at the pressing request of Bishop Vandevelde. It was to cover Illinois, as much as we could, with Roman Catholics from Canada, France, and Belgium, that we might put that splendid State, which was then a kind of wilderness, under the control of the Church of Rome. I then inquired from a priest about the particulars of the death of the late Bishop. That priest had no reasons whatever to deceive me and concede the truth, and it was with an evidently distressed mind that he gave the following details, which he assured me, were the exact, though very sad, truth:

"The Grand Vicar, M . . ., had fallen in love with his beautiful penitent, the accomplished Nun, . . . , Superioress of the Convent of Lorette. The consequence was that to conceal her fall, she went, under the pretext of recruiting her health, to a western city, where she soon died when giving birth to a dead-born child."

Though these mysteries of iniquity had been, as much as possible, kept secret, enough of them had come to the ears of the Bishop to induce him to tell the confessor that he was obliged to make inquiry about his conduct, and that, if found guilty, he would be interdicted. That priest boldly and indignantly denied his guilt; and said that he was glad of that inquiry. For he boasted that he was sure to prove his innocence. But after more mature deliberation, he changed his mind. In order to save his bishop the troubles of that inquiry, he administered to him a dose of poison which relieved him from the miseries of life, after five or six days of suffering which the doctors took for a common disease!!!

Auricular confession! These are some of thy mysteries!

The people of Detroit, Michigan, have not yet forgotten that amiable priest who was the confessor, "á la mode," of the young and old Roman Catholic ladies. They all remember still, the dark night during which he left for Belgium, with one of his most beautiful penitents, and $4,000 which he had taken from the purse of his Bishop Lefebvre, to pay his traveling expenses. And, who, in that same city of Detroit does not still sympathize with that young doctor whose beautiful wife eloped with her father confessor, in order, we must charitably suppose, to be more benefited when in the constant company of her spiritual and holy (?) physician.

Let my readers come with me to Bourbonnais Grove, and there, every one will show them the son whom the Priest Courjeault had from one of his fair penitents.

Weak-kneed Protestants! who are constantly speaking of peace, peace, with Rome, and who keep yourselves humbly prostrated at their feet, in order to sell them your wares, or get their suffrages, do you not understand your supreme degradation?

Do not answer to us that these are exceptional cases, for I am ready to prove that this unspeakable degradation and immorality are the normal state of the greater part of the priests of Rome. Father Hyacinthe has publicly declared, that ninety-nine out of one hundred of them, live in sin with the females they have destroyed. And not only the common priests are, for the greater part, sunk in that bottomless pit of secret or public infamy, but the bishops and popes, with the cardinals, are no better.

Who does not know the history of that interesting young girl of Armidale, Australia, who, lately, confessed to her distracted parents, that her seducer had been no less than a bishop! And when the enraged father prosecuted the bishop for damages, yes, is it not a public fact that he got £350 from the Pope's bishop, with the condition that he would emigrate with his family, to San Francisco, where this great iniquity might be concealed! But, unfortunately for the criminal confessor, the girl gave birth to a little bishop, before she left, and I can give the name of the priest who baptized the child of his own holy (?) and venerable (?) bishop.

Will the people of Australia ever forget the history of Father Nihills, who was condemned to three years in the penitentiary, for an unmentionable crime with one of his penitents?

This brings to my mind the deplorable end of Father Cahill, who cut his own throat not long ago, in New England, to escape the prosecution of the beautiful girl whom he had seduced. Who has not heard of that grand Vicar of Boston, who, about three years ago, poisoned himself to escape the sentence which was to be hurled against him the very next day, by the Supreme Court for having seduced one of his fair penitents?

Has not all France been struck with horror and confusion at the declarations made by the noble Catherine Cadière and her numerous young female friends, against their father confessor, the Jesuit, John B. Girard? The details of the villainies practiced by that holy (?) father confessor and his coadjutors, with their fair penitents, are such, that no Christian pen can retrace them, and no Christian reader would consent to have them put before his eyes.

If this chapter was not already long enough, I would say how Father Achazius, superior of a nunnery in Duren, France, used to sanctify the young and old ladies who confessed to him. The number of his victims was so great, and their ranks in society so exalted, that Napoleon thought it was his duty to take that scandalous affair before him.

The way this holy (?) father confessor used to lead the noble girls, married women, and nuns, of the territory of Aix-la-Chapelle, was revealed by a young nun who had escaped from the snares of the priest, and married a superior officer in the army of the Emperor of France. Her husband thought it his duty to direct the attention of Napoleon to the performances of that priest, through the confessional. But the investigations which were directed by the State Counsellor, Le Clerq, and the Professor Gall, were compromising so many other priests, and so many ladies in the highest ranks of society, that the Emperor was absolutely disheartened, and feared that their exposure before the whole of France, would cause the people to renew the awful slaughters of 1792 and 1793, when thirty thousand priests, monks and nuns, had been mercilessly hung, or shot dead, as the most implacable enemies of public morality and liberty. In those days, that ambitious man was in need of the priests to forge the fetters by which the people of France would be securely tied to the wheels of his chariot.

He abruptly ordered the court of investigation to stop the inquiry, under the pretext of saving the honor of so many families, whose single and married females had been seduced by their confessors. He thought that prudence and shame were urging him not to lift up more of the dark and thick veil, behind which the confessors conceal their hellish practices with their fair penitents. He found it was enough to confine Father Achazius and his co-priests in a dungeon for their lives.

But if we turn our eyes from the humble confessor priests to the monsters whom the Church of Rome adores as the vicars of Jesus Christ—the supreme Pontiffs—the Popes, do we not find horrors and abominations, scandals and infamies, which surpass everything which is done by the common priests behind the impure curtains of the confessional-box?

Does not Cardinal Baronius himself, tell us that the world has never seen anything comparable to the impurities and unmentionable vices of a great number of popes?

Do not the annals of the Church of Rome give us the history of that celebrated prostitute of Rome, Marozia, who lived in public concubinage with the Pope Sergius III., whom she raised to the so-called chair of St. Peter? Had she not also, by that Pope a son, of whom she also made a pope after the death of his holy (?) father, Pope Sergius?

Did not the same Marozia and her sister, Theodora, put on the pontifical throne another one of their lovers, under the name of Anastasius III., who was soon followed by John X.? And is it not a public fact, that that pope having lost the confidence of his concubine Marozia, was strangled by her order? Is it not also a fact of public notoriety, that his follower, Leo VI., was assassinated by her, for having given his heart to another woman, still more degraded?

The son whom Marozia had by Pope Sergius, was elected pope, by the influence of his mother, under the name of John XI., when not sixteen years old! But having quarrelled with some of the enemies of his mother, he was beaten and sent to gaol, where he was poisoned and died.

In the year 936, the grandson of the prostitute Marozia, after several bloody encounters with his opponents, succeeded in taking possession of the pontifical throne under the name of John XII. But his vices and scandals became so intolerable, that the learned and celebrated Roman Catholic Bishop of Cremorne, Luitprand, says of him:—"No honest lady dared to show herself in public, for the Pope John had no respect either for single girls, married women, or widows—they were sure to be defiled by him, even on the tombs of the holy apostles, Peter and Paul."

That same John XII. was instantly killed by a gentleman, who found him committing the act of adultery with his wife.

It is a well-known fact that Pope Boniface VII. had caused John XIV. to be imprisoned and poisoned, and when he soon after died, the people of Rome dragged his naked body through the streets, and left it, when horribly mutilated, to be eaten by dogs, if a few priests had not secretly buried him.

Let the readers study the history of the celebrated Council of Constance, called to put an end to the great schism, during which three popes, and sometimes four, were every morning cursing each other and calling their opponents Antichrists, demons, adulterers, sodomists, murderers, enemies of God and man.

As every one of them was an infallible pope, according to the last Council of the Vatican, we are bound to believe that they were correct in the compliments they paid to each other.

One of these holy (?) popes, John XXIII., having appeared before the Council to give an account of his conduct, he was proved by thirty-seven witnesses, the greater part of whom were bishops and priests, of having been guilty of fornication, adultery, incest, sodomy, simony, theft, and murder. It was proved also by a legion of witnesses, that he had seduced and violated 300 nuns. His own secretary, Niem, said that he had at Boulogne, kept a harem, where not less than 200 girls had been the victims of his lubricity.

And what could we not say of Alexander VI.? That monster who lived in public incest with his two sisters and his own daughter Lucretia, from whom he got a child.

But I stop—I blush to be forced to repeat such things. I would never have mentioned them were it not necessary not only to put an end to the insolence and the pretensions of the priests of Rome, but also to make the Protestants remember why their heroic fathers have made such great sacrifices and fought so many battles, shed their purest blood and even died, in order to break the fetters by which they were bound to the feet of the priests and the popes of Rome.

Let not my readers be deceived by the idea that the popes of Rome in our days, are much better than those of the ninth, tenth, eleventh and twelfth centuries. They are absolutely the same—the only difference is that, to-day, they take a little more care to conceal their secret orgies. For they know well, that the modern nations, enlightened as they are, by the light of the Bible, would not tolerate the infamies of their predecessors; they would hurl them very soon into the Tiber, if they dared to repeat in the open day, the scenes of which the Alexanders, Stephens, Johns, &c., &c., were the heroes.

Go to Italy, and there the Roman Catholics themselves will show you the two beautiful daughters whom the last pope, Pius IX., had from two of his mistresses. They will tell you, too, the names of five other mistresses—three of them nuns—he had when a priest and a bishop; some of them are still living.

Inquire from those who have personally known Pope Gregory XVI., the predecessor of Pius IX., and after they will have given you the history of his mistresses, one of whom was the wife of his barber, they will tell you that he was one of the greatest drunkards in Italy!

Who has not heard of the bastard, whom Cardinal Antonelli had from Countess Lambertini? Has not the suit of that illegitimate child of the great cardinal secretary filled Italy and the whole world with shame and disgust?

However, nobody can be surprised that the priests, the bishops, and the popes of Rome are sunk into such a bottomless abyss of infamy, when we remember that they are nothing else than the successors of the priests of Bacchus and Jupiter. For not only have they inherited their powers, but they have even kept their very robes and mantles on their shoulders, and their caps on their heads. Like the priests of Bacchus, the priests of the Pope are bound never to marry, by the impious and godless laws of celibacy. For every one knows that the priests of Bacchus were, as the priests of Rome, celibates. But, like the priests of the Pope, the priests of Bacchus, to console themselves for the restraints of celibacy, had invented auricular confession. Through the secret confidences of the confessional, the priests of the old idols, as well as those of the newly-invented wafer gods, knew who were strong and weak among their fair penitents, and under the veil "of the sacred mysteries," during the night celebration of their diabolical mysteries, they knew to whom they should address themselves, and make their vows of celibacy an easy yoke.

Let those who want more information on that subject read the poems of Juvenal, Propertius, and Tibellus. Let them peruse all the historians of old Rome, and they will see the perfect resemblance which exists between the priests of the Pope and those of Bacchus, in reference to the vows of celibacy, the secrets of auricular confession, celebration of the so-called "sacred mysteries," and the unmentionable moral corruption of the two systems of religion. In fact, when one reads the poems of Juvenal, he thinks he has before him the books of Den, Liguori, Lebreyne, Kenrick.

Let us hope and pray that the day may soon come when God will look in His mercy upon this perishing world; and then, the priests of the wafer gods, with their mock celibacy, their soul-destroying auricular confession and their idols will be swept away.

In that day Babylon—the great Babylon will fall, and heaven and earth shall rejoice.

For the nations will no more go and quench their thirst at the impure cisterns dug for them by the man of sin. But they will go and wash their robes in the blood of the Lamb; and the Lamb will make them pure by His blood, and free by His word. Amen.

CHAPTER XII

DENS wants the confessors to interrogate on the following matters:—

1. "Peccant uxores, quæ susceptum viri semen ejiciunt, vel ejicere conantur." (Dens, tom. vii., p. 147.)

2. "Peccant conjuges mortaliter, si, copulâ inceptâ, cohibeant seminationem."

3. "Si vir jam seminaverit, dubium fit an femina lethaliter peccat, si se retrahat a seminando; aut peccat lethaliter vir non expectando seminationem uxoris." (P. 153.)

4. "Peccant conjuges inter se circa actum conjugalom. Debet servari modus, sive situs; imo ut non servetur debitum vas, sed copula habeatur in vase præpostero, aliquoque non naturali. Si fiat accedendo a postero, a latere, stando, sedendo, vel si vir sit succumbus." (P. 166.)

5. "Impotentia est incapacitas perficiendi, copulum carnalem perfectam cum seminatione viri in vase debito seu, de se, aptam generationi. Vel, ut si mulier sit nimis arcta respectu unius viri, non respectu alterius." (Vol. vii., p. 273.)

6. "Notatur quod pollutio in mulieribus possit perfici, ita ut semen earum nou effluat extra membrum genitale.

"Indicium istius allegat Billuart, si scilicet mulier sensiat seminis resolutionem cum magno voluptatis sensu, qua completâ, passi satiatur." (Vol. iv., p. 168.)

7. "Uxor se accusans, in confessione, quod negaverit debitum, interrogetur an ex pleno rigore juirs sui id petiverit." (Vol. vii., p. 168.)

8. "Confessor pœnitentem, qui confitetur se pecasse cum sacerdote, vel sollicitatam ab eo od turpia, potest interrogare utrum ille sacerdos sit ejus confessarius, an in confessione sollitaverit." (Vol. vi., p. 294.)

There are a great many other unmentionable things on which Dens, in his fourth, fifth and seventh volumes, requires the confessor to ask his penitent, which I omit.

Now let us come to Liguori. That so-called Saint, Liguori, is not less diabolically impure than Dens, in his questions to the women. But I will cite only two of the things on which the spiritual physician of the Pope must not fail to examine his spiritual patient:—

1. "Quærat an sit semper mortale, si vir immitat pudenda in os uxoris?

"Verius affirmo quia, in hoc actu ob calorem oris, adest proximum periculum pollutionis, et videtur nova species luxuriæ contra naturam, dicta irruminatio."

2. "Eodem modo, Sanchez damnat virum de mortali, qui, in actu copulæ, immiteret dignitum in vas præposterum nxoris; quia, ut ait, in hoc actu adest affectus ad Sodomiam." (Liguori, tom. vi., p. 935.)

The celebrated Burchard, Bishop of Worms, has made a book of the questions which had to be put by the confessors to their penitents of both sexes. During several centuries it was the standard book of the priests of Rome. Though that work today is very scarce, Dens, Liguori, Debreyne, &c., &c., have ransacked its polluting pages, and given them to study to the modern confessors, in order to question their penitents. I will select only a few questions of the Roman Catholic Bishop to the young men:—

1. "Fecisti solus tecum fornicationem ut quidam facere solent; ita dico ut ipse tuum membrum virile in manum tuam acciperes, et sic duceres præputium tuum, et manu propria commoveres, ut sic, per illam delectationem semen projiceres?"

2. "Fornicationem fecisti cum masculo intra coxes; ita dicto ut tuum virile membrum intra coxas alterius mitteres, et sic agitando semen funderes?"

3. "Fecisti fornicationem, ut guidem facere solent, ut tuum virile membrum in lignum perforatum, aut in aliquod hujus modi mitteres, et, sic, per illam commotionem et delectationem semen projiceres?"

4. "Fecisti fornicationem contra naturam, id est, cum masculis vel animalibus coire, id est cum equo, cum vaccâ, vel asina, vel aliquo animali?" (Vol. i., p. 136.)

Among the questions we find in the compendium of the Right Rev. Burchard, Bishop of Worms, which must be put to women, are the following (p. 115):—

1. "Fecisti quod quædem mulieres solent, quodam molimen, au machinamentum in modum virilis membri ad mensbram tuæ voluptatis, et illud lodo verendorum tuorum aut alterius cum aliquibus ligaturis, ut fornacationem facereres cum aliis mulieribus, vel alia eodem instrumento, sive alio tecum?"

2. "Fecisti quod quædem mulieres facere solent ut jam supra dicto molimine, vel alio aliquo machinamento, tu ipsa in te solam faceres fornicationem?"

3. "Fecisti quod quædam mulieres facere solent, quando libidenem se vexantem exinguere volunt, quæ se conjungunt quasi coire debeant ut possint, et conjungunt invicem puerperia sua, et sic, fricando pruritum illarum extinguere desiderant?"

4. "Fecisti quod quædam mulieres facere solent, ut succumberes aliquo jumento et illiud jumentum ad coitum quolicumque posses ingenio,ut sic coiret tecum?"

The celebrated Debréyne has written a whole book, composed of the most incredible details of impurities, to instruct the young confessors in the art of questioning their penitents. The name of the book is "Mœchialogy," or "Treaty on all the sins against the sixth (seventh) and the ninth commandments, as well as on all the questions of the married life which refer to them."

That work is much approved and studied in the Church of Rome. I do not know that the world has ever seen anything comparable to the filthy and infamous details of that book. I will cite only two of the questions which Debréyne wants the confessor to put to his penitent:—

Of the young men (page 95) the confessor will ask:—

"Ad cognoscendum an usque ad pollutionem se tetigerent, quando tempore et quo fine se tetigerint; an tunc quosdam motus in corpore experti fuerint, et per quantum temporis spatium; an cessantibus tactibus, nihil insolitum et turpe accideret; an non longe majorem in compore voluptatem perceperint in fine tactuum quam in eorum principio; an tum in fine quando magnam delectationem carnalem sensuerunt, omnes motus corporis cessaverint; an non madefacti fuerint?" &c., &c.

Of the girl the confessor will ask:—

"Quæ sese tetegisse fatentur, an non aliquem puritum extinguere entaverint, et utrum pruritus ille cessaverit cam magnum senserint voluptatem; an tunc, ipsimet tactus cessaverint?" &c., &c.

The Right Rev. Kenrick, late Bishop of Boston, United States, in his book for the teaching of confessors on what matters they must question their penitents, has the following, which I select among thousands as impure and damnable to the soul and body:—

"Uxor quæ, in usu matrimonii, se vertit, ut non recipiat semen, vel statim post illud acceptum surgit ut expellatur, lethalitur peccat; sed opus non est ut diu resupina jaceat, quum matrix, brevi, semen attrahat, et mox, arctissime claudatur." (Vol. iii., p. 317.)

"Pullæ patienti licet se vertere, et conari ut non recipiat semen, quod injuria ei immittitur; sed, exceptum, non licet expellere, quia jam possessionem pacificam habet, et haud absque injuria naturæ ejiceretur." (Tom. iii., p. 317.)

"Conjuges senes plerumque coeunt absque culpa, licet contingat semen extra vas effudi; id enim per accidens fit ex infirmitate naturæ. Quod si véres adeo sint fractæ ut nullo sit seminandi intrevas spes, jam nequeunt jure conjugii uti." (Tom. iii., p. 317.)

THE BIBLE SAYS JESUS CHRIST SHED HIS PRECIOUS BLOOD ON THE CROSS SO THAT YOUR SINS COULD BE WASHED AWAY AND FORGIVEN. TO BE FORGIVEN, SAVED AND *KNOW* WE ARE GOING TO HEAVEN, THE BIBLE SHOWS US WHAT WE MUST DO:

HEARING THE WORD OF GOD ... *"So then faith cometh by hearing, and hearing by the word of God."* Romans 10:17

KNOWLEDGE ... *"Then said Jesus to those . . . which believed on him, If ye continue in my word . . . ye shall know the truth, and the truth shall make you free."* John 8:31, 32

BELIEVE ... *"For by grace are ye saved through* faith; *and that not of yourselves: it is the gift of God:* Not of works, *lest any man should boast."* Ephesians 2:8, 9

CONFESSION ... *"if thou shalt* confess *with thy mouth the Lord Jesus, and shalt* believe *in* thine heart . . . *thou shalt be saved. For with the* heart *man believeth unto righteousness; and with the mouth confession is made unto salvation."* Romans 10:9, 10

REPENT ... *"For godly sorrow worketh repentance to salvation . . . but the sorrow of the world worketh death."* II Corinthians 7:10

NOW THAT YOU ARE SAVED IN CHRIST, YOU ARE A CHILD OF GOD AND ON YOUR WAY TO HEAVEN. THE NEXT STEPS IN OBEDIENCE ARE:

BAPTISM ... *"*He that believeth *(first) and is baptized* shall be saved; *but he that believeth not shall be damned."* Mark 16:16

MEMBERSHIP IN A *BIBLE BELIEVING* CHURCH ... *"I will praise the Lord with my whole heart, in* the assembly *of the upright, and in the* congregation." Psalm 111:1

"Not forsaking the assembling of ourselves together, as the manner of some is; but exhorting one another . . ." Hebrews 10:25

GOD WILL NEVER LEAVE YOU NOR FORSAKE YOU (Hebrews 13:5) BECAUSE HE WILL BE IN YOUR HEART. THIS IS THE PROMISE TO YOU WHO ARE REALLY SAVED . . . AND THIS IS WHAT HE HAS GIVEN YOU.

YOU HAVE RECEIVED THE HOLY SPIRIT ... *"What? know ye not that your body is the temple of the Holy Ghost which is in you, which ye have of God, and ye are not your own?"* I Corinthians 6:19

YOU HAVE BEEN SEALED WITH THE HOLY SPIRIT ... Christ *"In whom ye also trusted, after that ye heard the word of truth, the gospel of your salvation: in whom also after that ye believed, ye were* sealed *with that Holy Spirit of promise."* Ephesians 1:13

YOU HAVE BEEN BAPTIZED INTO THE BODY OF CHRIST ... *"For by one Spirit are we* all *baptized into one body . . . and have been all made to drink into one Spirit."* I Corinthians 12:13

YOU WILL BE LED BY THE HOLY SPIRIT IN YOUR DAILY WALK ... *"Howbeit when he, the Spirit of truth, is come,* he will guide you *into* all truth: *for he shall not speak of himself; but whatsoever he shall hear, that shall he speak: and he will shew you things to come."* John 16:13

These things have I written unto you that believe on the name of the Son of God; that ye may KNOW *that ye have* ETERNAL LIFE, *and that ye may (continue to) believe on the name of the Son of God."* I John 5:13